THE BUILDER BOOK
NEW HAVEN PRESERVATION TRUST

© 2022

NHPT The New Haven Preservation Trust
ALL RIGHTS RESERVED
ISBN 979-8-218-02553-3

Pictures on the foregoing pages show construction by The Sperry & Treat Co. on York Street, New Haven, in May, 1926. The building under construction is now part of Jonathan Edwards College. The firm's founders, Nehemiah Sperry and Arthur Treat, are featured in this book.

Images courtesy of Yale University: Photographs (RU 608), Manuscripts and Archives, Yale University Library.

NHPT receives support from the State Historic Preservation Office of the Department of Economic and Community Development with funds from the Community Investment Act of the State of Connecticut.

THE BUILDER BOOK

CARPENTERS, MASONS AND CONTRACTORS IN HISTORIC NEW HAVEN

A PUBLICATION OF THE NEW HAVEN PRESERVATION TRUST

by Susan Godshall and Jack Tripp
Introduction by Christopher Wigren

PREFACE

NEW HAVEN, CONNECTICUT

This book is grounded in the New Haven Historic Resources Inventory (HRI), a collection of well-researched information sheets about 5,000 (more or less) historic structures in New Haven, Connecticut. Most of the HRI pages say "this building was built *for* so-and-so," often a businessman or manufacturer. A very few pages say "this building was built *by* so-and so," naming a carpenter or mason. This curious distinction led us to look up builders referred to in the HRI, which led to the idea of showcasing some of those builders, which led to months of searching for the life stories of past-century carpenters and masons.

The book features 23 builders who worked between 1810 and 1930, along with illustrations of their work. The selection of builders was defined by what exists in old records. We have accepted that there are builders named in the HRI and in architectural guides for whom few biographical details can be found. These 23 are not necessarily the most important; they are the ones that history has preserved.

For the featured buildings, we sought a mix of neighborhoods, architectural styles, and trades: carpenters, masons and a few real estate developers. One might wish for better representation of race and gender, but the present cannot change the past.

The Board of the New Haven Preservation Trust is grateful to the Connecticut State Historic Preservation Office for supporting this unusual publication idea. Thanks go to Executive Director Margaret Anne Tockarshewsky and Librarian Ed Surato at the New Haven Museum, without whose help this project would have been impossible. Staff at the Institute Library and the New Haven Free Public Library were generous with their time. Special thanks are owed to Christopher Wigren who patiently read draft after draft, making thoughtful suggestions. Karin Krochmal gently managed our schedule and matched it to the skills of the graphic designer Mark Zurolo. Channing Harris and Sandra Markham helped find 200-year-old news articles and Jean Pogwizd cheerfully took hundreds of pictures to illustrate over 50 structures.

Jack and I may have made mistakes in dates or addresses, and for that we apologize. We hope you will enjoy learning about many of the men—and a woman—who shaped our City.

Susan Godshall

CONTENTS

PAGE		
12	**Introduction**	
	Christopher Wigren	
17	**Nahum Hayward**	
	(1790–1847)	
①	143 Elm Street	
②	46 Hillhouse Avenue	
③	Fence around the Green	
25	**Elihu Atwater**	
	(1786–1875)	
④	Street Building	
	(742 Chapel Street)	
31	**William Lanson**	
	(c1785–1851)	
⑤	Long Wharf Pier	
39	**Simeon Jocelyn**	
	(1799–1879)	
⑥	Fence around Trowbridge Square	
⑦	32 Walnut Street and Jocelyn Square	
47	**Atwater Treat**	
	(1801–1882)	
⑧	106 Goffe Street	
⑨	Exchange Building (121 Church Street)	
⑩	250 Church Street	
55	**Sidney Mason Stone**	
	(1803–1882)	
⑪	37–39 Wooster Place	
⑫	311 Temple Street	
⑬	169 Olive Street	
⑭	55 Hillhouse Avenue	
65	**Stephen P. Perkins**	
	(1807–1890)	
⑮	1032 Chapel Street	
⑯	Trinity Chapel (301 George Street)	
⑰	Street Hall (1071 Chapel Street)	
⑱	393 Prospect Street	
73	**James E. English**	
	(1812–1890)	
⑲	9 Wooster Place	
⑳	592 Chapel Street	

81	**Philo Chatfield**
	(1819–1890)
㉑	66 Lyon Street
㉒	245 Greene Street
㉓	Battell Chapel (400 College Street)
89	**Massena Clark**
	(1811–1890)
㉔	86 Hallock Street
㉕	315 St. Ronan Street
97	**Willis M. Smith**
	(1819–1896)
㉖	399 Orange Street
㉗	Wolf's Head (77 Prospect Street)
㉘	Soldiers and Sailors Monument, East Rock Park
105	**Nehemiah D. Sperry**
	(1827–1911)
㉙	466 Orange Street
㉚	42 Academy Street
㉛	405-415 Orange Street
㉜	28-36 Trumbull Street
115	**Arthur B. Treat**
	(1853–1913)
㉝	466 Howard Avenue
㉞	37 High Street
123	**Lyman V. Treat**
	(1821–1896)
㉟	840 Howard Avenue
	George M. Treat
	(1856–1910)
㊱	836 Howard Avenue
129	**George P. Merwin**
	(1828–1905)
㊲	22 Eld Street
㊳	938 Grand Avenue (135–139 Olive St.)
135	**George A. Baldwin**
	(1830–1903)
㊴	297 Howard Avenue
㊵	333 Howard Avenue
㊶	217 Howard Avenue

143	**Charles M. McLinn**
	(1833–1906)
㊷	Farnam Hall (380 College Street)
㊸	Durfee Hall (198 Elm Street)
149	**George Bohn**
	(1848–1915)
㊹	Quinnipiac Brewery (21 River Street)
㊺	21 Kossuth Street
157	**Thomas F. Lowe**
	(1851–1888)
㊻	338–340 Grand Avenue
㊼	342–346 Grand Avenue
㊽	350 Grand Avenue
163	**Ettore Frattari**
	(c1867–1954)
㊾	748–752 Elm Street
㊿	742 Elm Street
169	**Alice T. Washburn**
	(1870–1958)
51	86 Elmwood Road
52	30 Alston Avenue
53	11 Alden Avenue
177	**Vito Zichichi**
	(1876–1951)
54	13–15, 17–19, 21–23, 27–29 and 31–33 Blake Street
55	409 Ellsworth Avenue
183	**Index**
189	**Sources**

INTRODUCTION

Architectural history has long focused on architects and clients, and New Haven has a long history of visionary architects and sophisticated clients who together created a rich architecture. But that leaves out another crucial group—the builders who translated architects' plans and clients' wishes into actual structures. This book takes the first step in identifying and telling the stories of some significant figures in that industry and their part creating the New Haven of today.

New Haven grew and changed dramatically in the nineteenth and early twentieth centuries, and the building industry grew and changed along with it. Between 1800 and 1930, the city's economy transitioned from shipping and handcrafts to manufacturing. Rapid population growth followed, from 5,157 in 1800 to 162,655 in 1930. At the same time, New Haven's ethnic makeup changed from overwhelmingly white, Protestant, and of English ancestry to a mix of ethnic groups and religions. In 1930, nearly one-quarter of the city's residents had been born elsewhere, 26 percent of that number in Italy. Another 3 percent was Black, a number that would continue to grow as the Great Migration from the South continued.

This growing population needed to be housed. In 1850, New Haven possessed 5,353 dwellings; by 1910 the figure was 17,466, about two-thirds of them in multi-unit structures. Schools, churches, commercial, civic, and industrial buildings also were needed. To meet these needs, the demand for builders grew steadily.

In this context, many builders became prominent and respected citizens, the possessors of valuable skills. They knew about *construction*—how to put a building together so that it could accommodate various needs and stand firm. They knew about *management*—how to estimate and source materials, how to recruit and coordinate skilled workers. And they knew about *finances*—how to determine the cost of a building, pay for the materials and labor, and make a profit. These qualities often were seen as translatable to other community needs, and so successful builders were often chosen for positions of public trust.

Many of these biographical sketches show how success in building led to social recognition and advancement, and opportunities for public service. The twenty-three builders portrayed here include elected or appointed officials—at city, state, and federal levels—as well as directors of nonprofit organizations and industrial or financial businesses, church leaders, and militia officers. Immigrant builders such as Thomas Lowe became assimilated in the community and built dozens of houses and factories.

Opportunities for Blacks proved more limited but were not unheard of. William Lanson was a leader of the Black community until he was undone by jealous whites, while Charles McLinn enjoyed long-term employment as head carpenter at Yale and filled several elective or appointed civic roles.

Manufacturing contributed to a second change in New Haven's building industry. In 1800 nearly everything that went into a structure was made at or near the site, but by the end of the century, building materials increasingly were mass produced. The availability of ready-made components speeded construction while reducing demand for certain skills. Some New Haven builders expanded into manufacturing, such as George P. Merwin and William R. Hubbell who opened a shop to produce millwork.

A third change was the emergence of architecture as a profession distinct from construction. In 1800, master builders conceived and constructed buildings, perhaps consulting a builder's guide for details such as classical orders or tricky construction problems such as curved stairs. Occasionally, an educated amateur would design a building, but that rarely entailed more than a floorplan and an elevation, created with the expectation that the builder would fill in the details. The first professional architect to open an office in New Haven was Sidney Mason Stone, in 1833. Others soon joined him, and by the 1860s plans by professional architects were the rule for public buildings, churches, and ambitious private residences.

Some builders followed Stone's lead and became architects, generally by apprenticing themselves to another architect, or by buying a shelf full of pattern books and simply proclaiming themselves to be architects. Others worked mostly from professionally drawn plans, as Stephen Perkins and Philo Chatfield did. Still others continued to build in the old, vernacular way, creating their own plans, modifying architects' designs, or adapting ideas from patternbooks. Historian Thomas Hubka observes that, well into the twentieth century, most working-class housing was constructed by small-scale contractor-builders like Vito Zichichi. Through the century, the lines between these three groups—and between builders and architects—remained fluid. An example of this fluidity might be Alice Washburn, who acted as an architect to design houses, but also assembled a crew of workers to build her designs.

In addition to builders and contractors, developers were key to New Haven's evolution. Some, like Massena Clark and Simeon Jocelyn, never worked as builders. But builders themselves could be well placed to become developers: they had the knowledge and crews to construct speculative buildings without having to pay a separate builder's profits. Several builders included in this book went into development at various levels: Sidney Mason Stone, Simeon Jocelyn, Ettore Frattari, and others.

But how exactly did builders interact with architects and customers to produce New Haven's buildings? The principal sources for these biographical sketches, local histories from the late nineteenth or early twentieth centuries, are frustratingly quiet about that. What is needed are diaries, account books, correspondence, or building committee records that can put flesh on the bones of a project or a career. J. Ritchie

Garrison provides an example from another state. Perhaps some lucky reader will discover a similar source for a New Haven builder.

Until that happens, the entries here give us *names*, ensuring that New Haven's builders will not sleep in obscurity. They also remind us that these builders were important people in their community, and that they not only contributed to its built form but also were trusted with positions of responsibility. They were respected and remembered. We need to know more about them.

Christopher Wigren
Deputy Director
Preservation Connecticut

For further reading

Clouette, Bruce, and Matthew Roth.
"Villa Friuli." *National Register of Historic Places*,
reference number 91000349, listed 11 April 1991.

Garrison, J. Ritchie.
Two Carpenters: Architecture and Building in Early New England, 1799–1859.
Knoxville: University of Tennessee Press, 2006.

Hubka, Thomas C.
How the Working-Class Home Became Modern, 1900–1940.
Minneapolis and London: University of Minnesota Press, 2020.

NAHUM HAYWARD
1790–1847

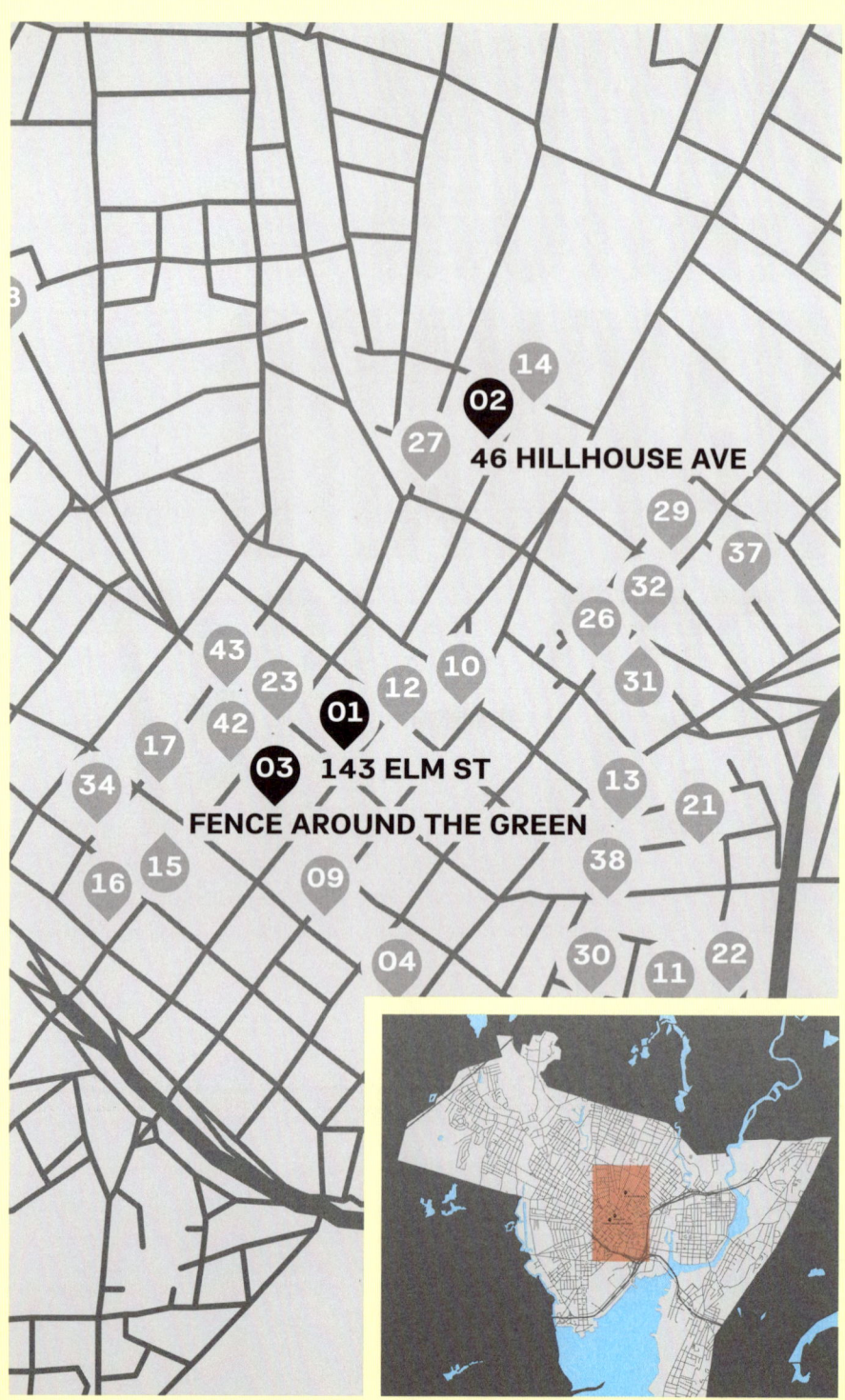

01

143 Elm Street

19 NAHUM HAYWARD

02 | 46 Hillhouse Avenue

03 | Fence around the Green

20   THE BUILDER BOOK   NEW HAVEN PRESERVATION TRUST

Nahum Hayward is one of the earliest carpenters in New Haven's written record. He was born in 1790 in Bridgewater, Massachusetts and died in 1847 in New Haven, at age 56. He married Mary E. Dudley in 1824 and they had five children. The family lived on the east side of Church Street, just south of Grove Street.

Hayward was a member of the New Haven Common Council from 1832 to 1841. In 1834, he was appointed with five others to examine and survey the City's streets, assigned to "identify all obstructions and nuisances... and cause them to be removed."

Despite his slim recorded biography, Nahum Hayward built some of the most recognizable houses of his era, including the Ingersoll House facing the New Haven Green at 143 Elm Street, built in 1829 for the Hon. Ralph I. Ingersoll, elected as Mayor and U.S. Congressman and appointed as Ambassador to Russia.

The Ingersoll House was designed by Ithiel Town and Alexander Jackson Davis, whose firm established the Greek Revival style as the dominant form in the city's mid-century architecture. According to Elizabeth Mills Brown, of the 30 to 40 buildings in New Haven known to be designed by this firm, seven or eight remained at the time of Brown's 1976 book, mostly stripped of their original landscaping. Many builders featured in this book, Hayward among them, carried out Town & Davis designs and learned to copy and adapt them.

Despite his slim recorded biography, Nahum Hayward built some of the most recognizable houses of his era, including the Ingersoll House facing the New Haven Green at 143 Elm Street, built in 1829 for the Hon. Ralph I. Ingersoll, elected as Mayor and U.S. Congressman and appointed as Ambassador to Russia.

The Ingersoll House is an early Greek Revival dwelling with much of its exterior detail intact, despite many renovations over 192 years. The north side of the Green was an elegant residential sector throughout the nineteenth century. The house sits high on its foundation with symmetrical windows trimmed with stone headers and sills. A wide flight of steps leads to an imposing porch with Doric columns and a deep entablature. The fashionable Greek Revival style and high quality of the building materials conveyed then, as they do now, a luxurious statement at a prominent corner.

A year before the Ingersoll House, Hayward had built Sachem's Wood, James Abraham Hillhouse's mansion on the rise at the head of Hillhouse Avenue. Sachem's Wood was a grand Greek Revival structure, notable for park-like surroundings and a prominent site overlooking land all the way to the New Haven Green. Sachem's Wood stayed in the Hillhouse family until shortly before it was demolished in 1942.

Town & Davis evidently valued Nahum Hayward's skill; Hayward was also the builder in 1832 for the Aaron Skinner House (later the Trowbridge House) at 46 Hillhouse Avenue. Significantly altered over 190 years, it remains one of New Haven's most distinguished houses. Although Skinner only wanted a simple home for his boys' school, James A. Hillhouse, relying on funds from his wife's father, stepped in to enhance and enlarge the structure. The result, a Greek Revival mansion with a portico framed by four towering columns, cost the then-alarming sum of $6,300.

In 1846, Hayward was hired to set the iron and stone fence around the New Haven Green, a lasting improvement over the older, much-repaired wood fence. The cost of $6,850 was funded by the City treasury. Since the Statehouse was located on the Green at the time, financial assistance for the new fence was requested from the State but was not approved.

The ceremonial fence surrounding the Green remains one of its most recognizable features, although the name of its builder would be recognized by few residents. Yet Hayward was admired and respected in his day; his tombstone in Grove Street cemetery reads, *"Erected by his Masonic brothers & fellow citizens in respect to the memory of an honest man."*

ELIHU ATWATER 1786–1875

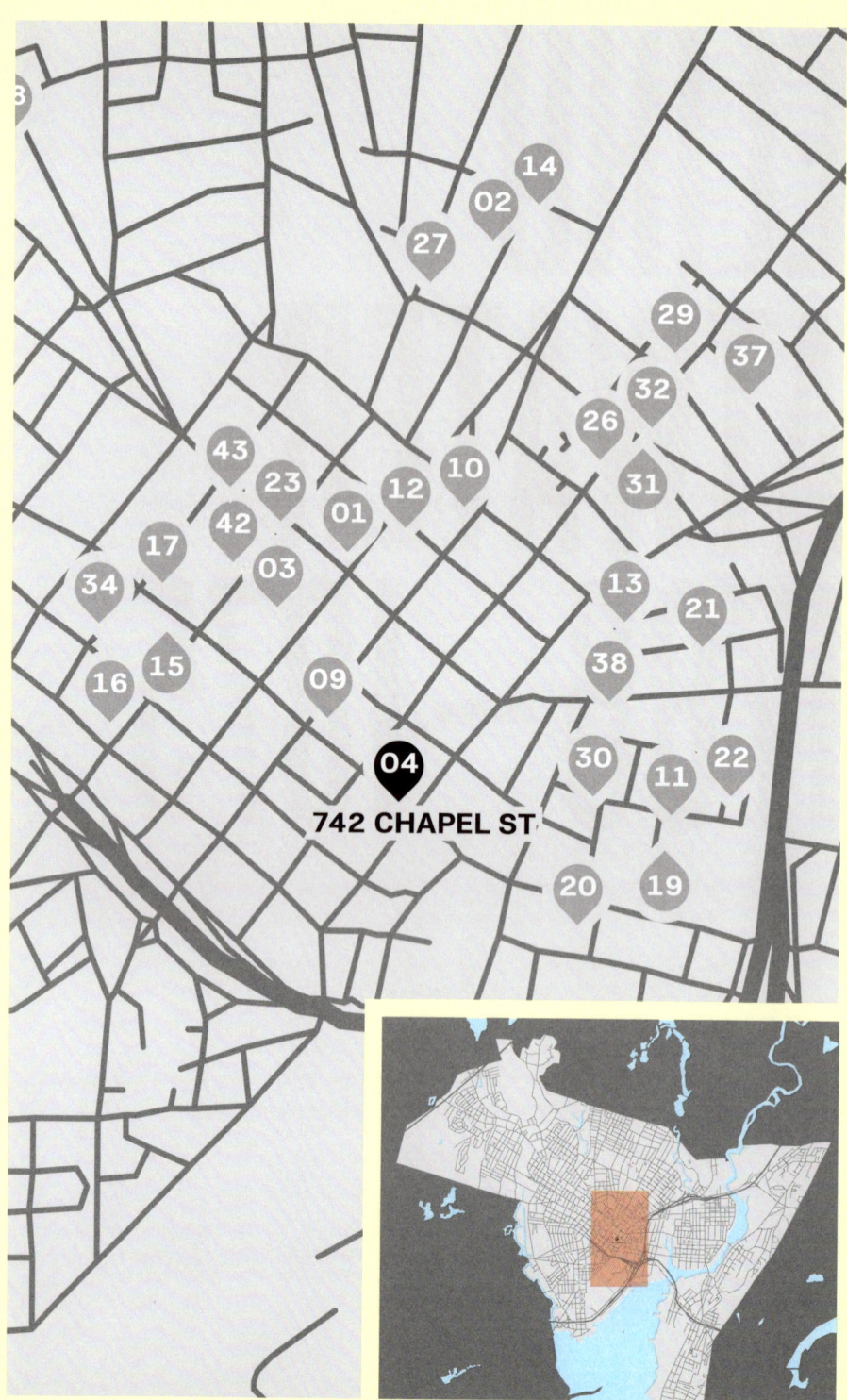

04 — 742 Chapel Street / Street Building

742 Chapel Street / Street Building

Elihu Atwater was born in December, 1786, in New Haven. He learned the masonry trade from his uncle, Elisha Dickerman, and spent a year when he was 22 years old working as a journeyman in "New Connecticut," which was the first name that Vermont adopted when it declared independence from the State of New York in 1777.

Atwater returned to New Haven in 1809 and opened a masonry business. He married Julia Thompson in 1811, and had four children, only one of whom, Edward Elias, lived to adulthood. [Edward is the author of the extensive *"History of the City of New Haven to the Present Time,"* published in 1887, which includes brief biographies of many of these builders.]

During the War of 1812, Elihu Atwater served in a volunteer militia called the New Haven Grays and helped build earthworks on the harbor to protect against an invasion from the sea. He recalled to a biographer years later that on one occasion, he and other volunteers saw the alarm flag, gathered in formation, and marched to the earthworks expecting a mortal battle, only to find that the British "frigate" seen by the signal men was a peaceful lumber ship.

Julia died in 1818 and Atwater married Betsy Tyler in 1819. He was elected to the Common Council in 1835 and served as a vice president of New Haven Savings Bank beginning in 1847.

Atwater owned land around Wooster Square Park and donated a parcel at 349 Greene Street for the new site of the Davenport Congregational Church, where his son Edward was the minister. The church was designed by Rufus G. Russell in 1874, but the record is not clear whether Atwater's firm participated in its construction.

Elihu Atwater died in 1875 at the age of 88 and is buried in Grove Street Cemetery.

Atwater is known today as the builder of the Street Building at the corner of Chapel and State Streets. Constructed in 1832, it is one of three early structures in New Haven that introduced a new building form conceived specifically for commercial use; the others are the Exchange—see Atwater Treat in this book—and the Townsend Block at Chapel and College Streets. The New Haven Historic Resources Inventory notes that "This building and its counterparts are very important to the commercial history of the City."

The Street Building is a large square masonry block, distinct from earlier commercial structures modeled on residential rowhouses. Its four stories provided rental space to many merchants under one roof. On the State Street side, original granite piers still outline where the shops would have opened to the street. Above, there are bands of tightly spaced windows with stone lintels and sills. The Chapel Street side was modified in 1921. The Street Building remains an important anchor at the eastern edge of downtown.

WILLIAM LANSON c.1785–1851

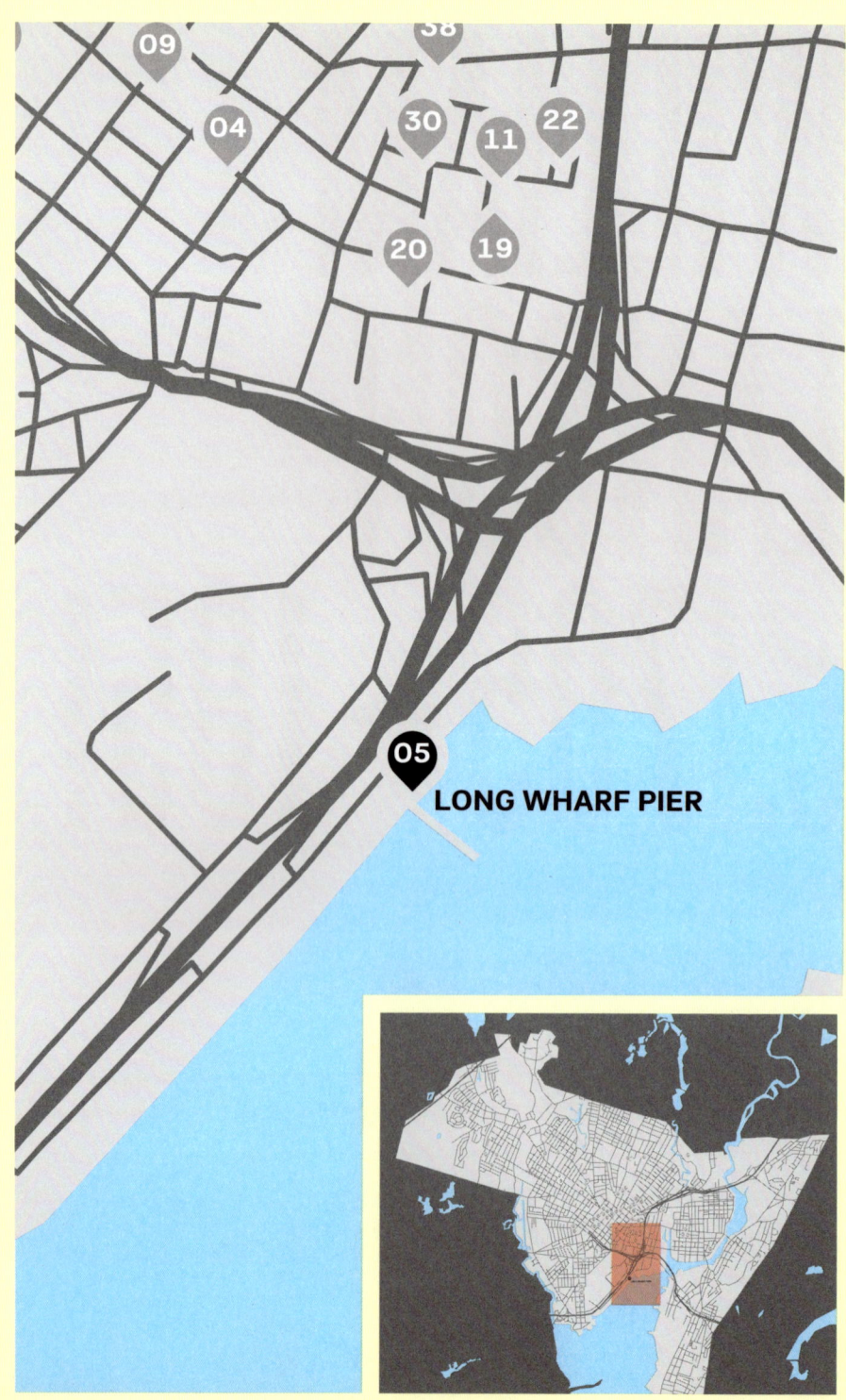

05 Long Wharf Pier

Long Wharf Pier

Recognition has grown in recent years for the remarkable achievements of self-taught engineer William Lanson. A free Black man probably born around 1785, Lanson and his family moved to New Haven about 1803. Within seven years, he had become the city's principal wharf builder, hired by investor and developer James Hillhouse in 1810 to extend Long Wharf pier out to the shipping channel in the harbor.

Long Wharf pier dates back to the late 1600s, as a dock built out from the creeks at the intersection of Union and Water Streets. For about 140 years, the dock did not reach the shipping channel and so could not service larger ships directly. Lanson convinced Hillhouse that he could extend the wharf into the harbor to make it useful for the expanding export trade. Lanson realized that the conventional method of building wharves on wooden piers would not provide enough support in the deep mud flats of New Haven harbor. He designed a means of bringing large stones downstream on flat scows that could each hold 25 tons, using stone as the structure of the wharf. This technique enabled him to extend Long Wharf by 1,325 feet—at the time, the longest wharf in the country. This solution to an enduring problem, together with his relentless drive to complete the project, were widely admired. The largest ships could be moored to the wharf at all stages of the tide,

Lanson owned and developed land in part of the New Township called New Guinea, at the northern edge of what is now Wooster Square. Later he sold those interests and bought land and buildings at the end of Greene Street, a district he called New Liberia. Lanson built houses, stores and a hotel in the area, providing opportunities to Blacks in New Haven at a time when most whites would not.

avoiding the need for them to anchor offshore and unload cargo onto lighter vessels to bring goods into port.

Lanson's neat brownstone rows can be seen today at low tide beneath the boulders installed during the construction of I-95. Without a doubt, Lanson's stonework enabled the success of New Haven's import/export trade in the first half of the nineteenth century.

In an 1811 report on the current state of New Haven, Yale University's Reverend Timothy Dwight praised Lanson's wharf work for the "honourable proof of [his] character, both for capacity and integrity, in the view of respectable men."

Along with others, Lanson was a founder of the City's first Black church, originally located on Temple Street, now known as Dixwell Avenue Congregational United Church of Christ. His other construction work included brownstone retaining walls for the Farmington Canal and the base of the first Tomlinson Bridge.

In the early 1800s, Lanson owned and developed land in part of the New Township called New Guinea, at the northern edge of what is now Wooster Square. Later he sold those interests and bought land and buildings at the end of Greene Street, a district he called New Liberia. Lanson built houses, stores and a hotel in the area, providing opportunities to Blacks in New Haven at a time when most whites would not. He hired Black workers, paid them fair wages, and fought for their suffrage. For a time, Lanson was reportedly the wealthiest Black man in the State and was called the Black Governor.

However, his success earned him harassment from business leaders and policemen. His hotel was raided and he was taken to court on trumped up charges and jailed several times. Sustained attacks on Lanson's economic and social success eventually brought down his enterprises and he died in poverty in 1851.

The City honored his achievements in the form of a public park near the Farmington Canal Line where a statue of Lanson was dedicated in 2020. Today there is widespread—though belated—recognition of Lanson's skills as an engineer, entrepreneur, and community leader.

SIMEON JOCELYN 1799–1879

07
32 WALNUT ST
AND JOCELYN SQUARE

06
FENCE AROUND
TROWBRIDGE SQUARE

40   THE BUILDER BOOK   NEW HAVEN PRESERVATION TRUST

06

Fence around Trowbridge Square

41 SIMEON JOCELYN

07 · 32 Walnut Street and Jocelyn Square

Simeon Jocelyn was an abolitionist, social reformer, and among the biggest real estate speculators in nineteenth century New Haven. Born in 1799, he and his brother Nathaniel devoted themselves to establishing racial justice for much of their lives.

Jocelyn started a profitable business engraving bank notes and studied for the ministry with tutors at Yale University. Beginning in 1820, he was the first pastor of a Black church on Temple Street called the United African Society, now the Dixwell Avenue Congregational United Church of Christ, and quickly became known as an advocate for human freedom.

He married Harriet Starr in 1822 and they had six children.

In an effort to offer higher education to Black students, Jocelyn proposed the formation of a Negro College in 1831, only to see his vision decisively rejected at the New Haven town meeting. The defeat of the Negro College proposal led to personal reprisals against Jocelyn, including a mob attack on his house.

In 1839, while captives from the *Amistad* ship were held in a New Haven jail, Jocelyn helped found an "Amistad Committee" to work outside the courtroom on the captives' behalf. Unverified accounts from the era name both Simeon and Nathaniel Jocelyn as conductors on the Underground Railroad for fugitives from the South.

"Mr. Jocelyn connected himself with anti-slavery organizations in the days when to be an abolitionist was the reverse of popular.... His policy was to discountenance all differences of race or condition."

Simeon Jocelyn and his family moved to Brooklyn in 1844; he continued to work in the ministry there until he died in 1879. His obituary said, "Mr. Jocelyn connected himself with anti-slavery organizations in the days when to be an abolitionist was the reverse of popular.... His policy was to discountenance all differences of race or condition."

Early in the 1830s, Jocelyn purchased land, laid out new streets, and developed a neighborhood now known as Trowbridge Square. He named the area "Spireworth" and hoped to create a model working-class community. Spireworth began as a nine-square grid, modeled after the layout of early New Haven, with a public open space in the center surrounded by iron and stone fencing in the same style as that of the Green. The street frontages were subdivided into building lots for the small frame houses which still characterize this area.

City Directories from the 1830s indicate that homes of Blacks and whites were integrated along Spireworth streets. Today, Trowbridge Square retains its distinguishing architectural character of compact, stylistically pared-down houses. The Trowbridge Square Historic District is the City's most intact and cohesive example of a nineteenth-century working-class residential area.

The Jocelyns' next real estate venture was even bigger. Simeon and Nathaniel bought a huge tract of land in 1835, from Grand Avenue north to State Street and from Hamilton Street east to the Mill River. With dozens of lots laid out for small houses intended for tradesmen and artisans, the development was an ambitious scheme that was only moderately successful. The depression of 1837–38 ended further real estate development by the Jocelyns.

The centerpiece of the second Jocelyn development was Franklin Square, now named Jocelyn Square. Once again, unlike developers from the era who catered to upper class buyers, Jocelyn's goal was to create a neighborhood for the working class. The house at the southeastern corner of Jocelyn Square, 32 Walnut Street, is one of the few remaining examples built before the Civil War. A 2½ story Greek Revival house, it has a gable with a full return across the front and an oversized doorway trimmed with two fluted columns and a wide frieze, originally trimmed with horizontal bands but now faced with siding laid in vertical strips.

Although not a hands-on builder, Simeon Jocelyn represents a bold approach to pre-Civil War development in New Haven, buying open land and overseeing design and construction of new neighborhoods of modest houses. Coupled with his commitment to the abolitionist cause, Jocelyn's contributions to New Haven are both physical and moral.

ATWATER TREAT 1801–1882

48   THE BUILDER BOOK   NEW HAVEN PRESERVATION TRUST

106 Goffe Street / Goffe Street School

49   ATWATER TREAT

09 — 121 Church Street / Exchange Building

10 — 250 Church Street

Like many builders of his era, Atwater Treat was not only an accomplished carpenter but also an active member of the New Haven community. Biographers give substantial attention to the civic roles held by successful nineteenth century carpenters, masons and contractors; their contributions included fire and police commissions, Federal appointments as postmasters, and State and local elected offices. From about 1830 to 1890, many carpenters and masons who owned or managed a business often had a leading role in the City's affairs.

Atwater Treat was born in Milford in January, 1801, and was apprenticed at age 17 to James Chaplin, the head carpenter for Yale College. Over his lifetime, Treat shared in the construction of many Yale buildings, most no longer standing. In 1827, he took on his own apprentice, a sixteen-year-old named James E. English (also included in this book) who later became a corporate and civic leader, U.S. Senator and Connecticut Governor.

In 1821, Treat was caught up in the fervor of the Second Great Awakening and joined North Church on the Green, now known as United Church. He supported several local charities and donated to Congregationalist missionaries with the profits from growing fields

An advocate for the underprivileged, Treat was appointed in 1862 to the Local Board of the Freedmen's Association, formed to provide relief and protection to freed Blacks living in Union territory during the Civil War.

of carrots on a vacant lot on York Street. He was chosen as Deacon of North Church in 1850 and held this position for the rest of his life.

Treat was a co-founder of the New Haven Young Men's Institute (today the Institute Library) and served on the New Haven City Council beginning in 1847. Late in life, he was a director of the Fair Haven & Westville Horse Railroad, a horse-drawn street car business that carried over 1,000,000 passengers a year. Treat was also a guarantor in an early arrangement to address the New Haven Hospital's deficits, joining with others with an annual subscription to cover hospital losses not made up by fees and donations.

Atwater Treat was married three times. His first wife, Betsy, died in 1840 at age 33 and his second wife, Elizabeth, died in 1849 at age 37. His third wife, Adeline, outlived him, dying in 1883. Of his five children, only one, James, lived past early childhood.

An advocate for the underprivileged, Treat was appointed in 1862 to the Local Board of the Freedmen's Association, formed to provide relief and protection to freed Blacks living in Union territory during the Civil War. In 1864, Treat and five others formed a plan to build a school for Black children, "in view of the fact that they have been less favored than others [in] educational advantages." This became the Goffe Street Special School, located at 106 Goffe Street, one of the most notable sites related to Black history in New Haven. A two-story brick structure, the building was reportedly designed at no charge by architect Henry Austin. The Goffe Street Special School served as a community center and school until 1929, and is listed on the National Register of Historic Places.

Atwater Treat died in March, 1882, and is buried in Grove Street Cemetery. His funeral sermon, delivered in North Church, extolled his buildings, which "stand bearing witness by their own symmetry and solidity, to the beauty and strength of character of him who built them."

Treat is best known as the builder in 1832 of the Exchange (121 Church Street) at the corner of Church and Chapel Streets, the center of New Haven's commercial district. Its brick construction suggests that Treat worked closely with a masonry crew or operated as what we would now call a general contractor. The ambitious design suggests that plans were drawn by an architect, possibly Ithiel Town, who would have seen similar commercial structures in New York and London.

The Exchange was the first structure in New Haven designed for multiple business rentals; its imposing 18-bay width along Church Street contributes to the ambience and dignity of the Green. A large 4-story Greek Revival block, it has entrances flanked by pilasters on both Church and Chapel Streets. The Exchange housed prominent businesses and institutions including the beginnings of what is now the New Haven Museum and the earliest documented theater in New Haven. For years, it was known as the site of a town/gown riot in 1854. The original cupola was lost and then happily replaced in the late 20th century.

In 1841 Atwater Treat built Theodore Woolsey's house at 250 Church Street, one of only two early residential structures remaining on upper Church Street. Woolsey was a professor of Greek when his house was built and was President of Yale University from 1846 to 1871. His house was originally five bays wide with chimneys at the gable ends. It was transformed into a neo-classical mansion in 1906, adding two bays, corner pilasters, and a wide pediment, but the original dimensions are defined by the location of the still-surviving chimneys. The Woolsey House was part of a fashionable residential neighborhood until the 1930s when commercial and institutional uses took over the area.

One of the first well-documented builders in New Haven, Atwater Treat lived a full life, aptly summarized in words from his eulogy, "He worked, prayed, and gave."

SIDNEY MASON STONE 1803–1882

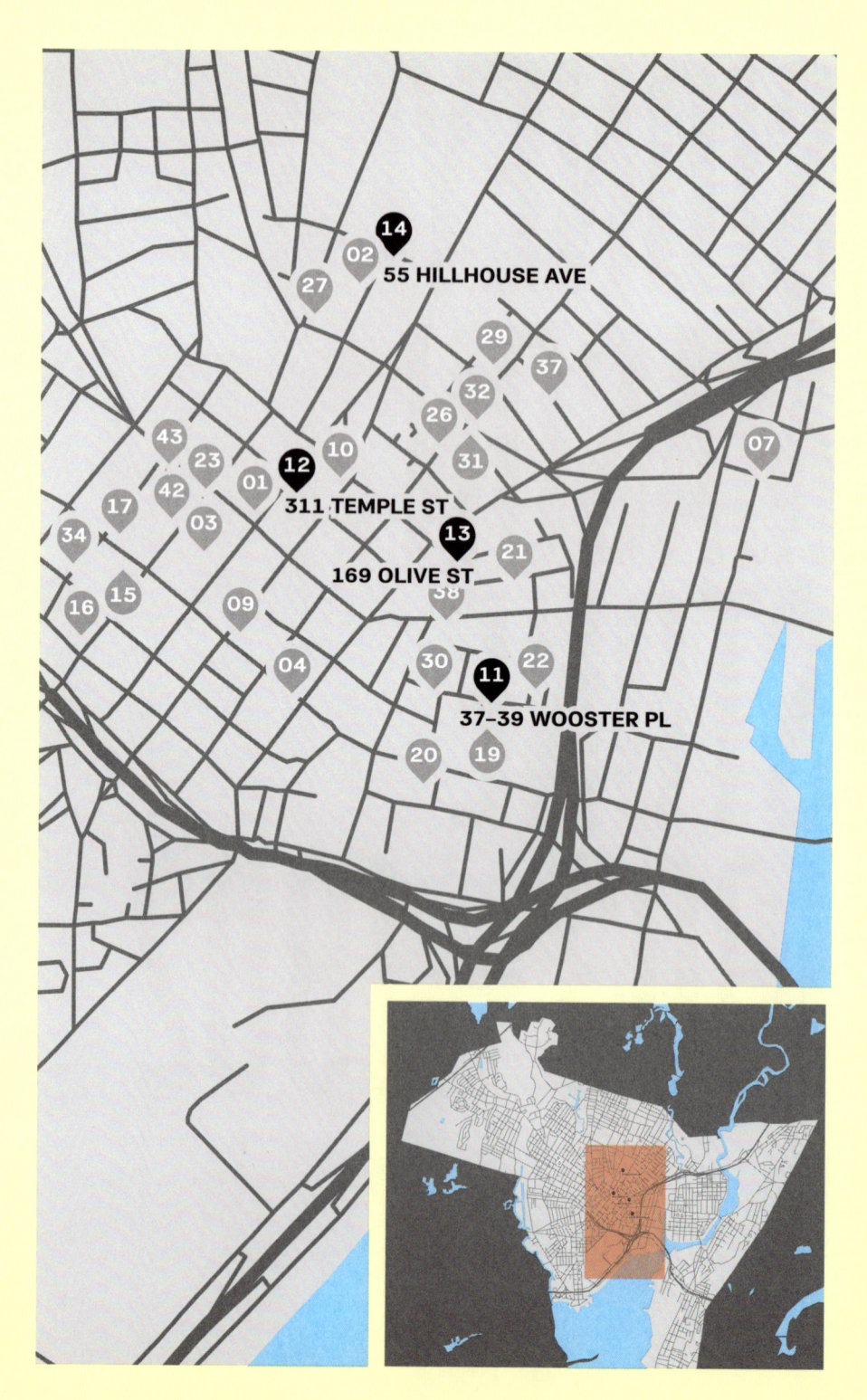

14 55 HILLHOUSE AVE
12 311 TEMPLE ST
13 169 OLIVE ST
11 37–39 WOOSTER PL

56   THE BUILDER BOOK   NEW HAVEN PRESERVATION TRUST

37–39 Wooster Place

12

311 Temple Street

58   THE BUILDER BOOK   NEW HAVEN PRESERVATION TRUST

169 Olive Street

59 SIDNEY MASON STONE

14

55 Hillhouse Avenue

Sidney Stone, a descendant of Mayflower Pilgrims, was born in Orange, Connecticut, in 1803 and came to New Haven in 1822. As a young man, he offered himself for hire as a carpenter or joiners. In 1832, Stone studied civil engineering at the newly-opened New York University and a year later began advertising his services in New Haven as a master builder. He married Abigail Treat in 1830, who died shortly after the birth of her fifth child. His second wife, Harriet Mulford, had two children. Stone's daughter Harriet became well known as the author of the popular *Five Little Peppers* young adult series, under the pen name of Margaret Sidney.

Stone served in many civic roles including four years as a town councilman and captain of a local defense force known as the New Haven Grays. He died in 1882 and is buried in Grove Street Cemetery.

Stone gradually moved away from hands-on building trades and adopted the role of architect. This book focuses on sites where Stone had a part in the construction, but at other times, in New Haven and elsewhere, he was exclusively a designer. Unfortunately, most of his drawings were destroyed after his death and his architectural library was sold.

Stone was a friendly rival to New Haven architect Henry Austin, a sought-after designer by the 1840s; contemporary records say that

Stone's earliest recorded commission was the brick house with a formal Greek Revival porch at 37-39 Wooster Place (1833), then the home of Mayor John B. Robertson. The house was built in the traditional five-bay configuration and later divided into two homes, indicated by the blind window above the entry.

Stone and Austin occasionally vied for the same projects. They served together on Mayor Harmanus Welch's Harbor Committee in 1863.

Stone's earliest recorded commission was the brick house with a formal Greek Revival porch at 37–39 Wooster Place (1833), then the home of Mayor John B. Robertson. The house was built in the traditional five-bay configuration and later divided into two homes, indicated by the blind window above the entry.

This project was followed by a number of houses incorporating Italianate, Greek Revival and Gothic features. Stone's appeal is based on his ability to shape these architectural movements into attractive variations. Existing examples include the John North House at 158 Whitney Avenue (c.1836), for which we have Stone's detailed specifications, the Ezekiel Trowbridge House (1852), and the Peletiah Perit House (1860).

The Ezekiel Trowbridge House at 311 Temple Street, now the Center Church Parish House, is a graceful Italianate villa with a flat roof and an intricately carved porch unlike any other in New Haven. Each of the oversized front windows is topped by brownstone headers with carved brackets. The fancy monitor was once seen through an open balustrade around the roof. A model of "foursquare symmetry," according to Elizabeth Mills Brown, the Ezekiel Trowbridge House extended a series of elegant houses on Elm Street, termed "Quality Row," around the corner onto Temple Street.

Eight years later, Stone used the same Italian villa form in the Peletiah Perit House at 55 Hillhouse Avenue but with a more disciplined approach. The house is taller, the cornice is deeper, and the porch and window treatments have been given Renaissance details. Now owned by Yale University, the Perit House is one of Stone's most distinguished achievements.

Starting in the 1830s, Stone acquired large land-holdings north of Grand Avenue, including acreage that he opened up for development as Lyon Street. He built his own house in 1848 at 169 Olive Street, at the corner of Lyon Street. Larger than many nearby houses, 169 Olive Street is masonry with a stucco surface. The Italianate detailing is typical of Stone's work, including a heavy cornice with brackets and a whimsical round window. Although the original entrance is obscured by a modern wall, the house is an important anchor at the northwest corner of the Wooster Square neighborhood.

In addition to his design skill, Stone had ample business acumen, with major real estate dealings in Fair Haven and in the Upper State Street area north of Humphrey Street. From his office in the Phoenix Building on Chapel Street, he purchased and sold lots for both residential and commercial use, making him a significant player in New Haven's expansion to the north and east in the 1850s and 1860s.

STEPHEN P. PERKINS 1807–1890

393 PROSPECT ST
STREET HALL
1032 CHAPEL ST
TRINITY CHAPEL

15 1032 Chapel Street

15 1032 Chapel Street

Gaius F. Warner House, built 1860. Henry Austin, architect. Image courtesy of the New Haven Museum.

16 — 301 George Street / Trinity Chapel

17 — 1071 Chapel Street / Street Hall

69   STEPHEN P. PERKINS

18

393 Prospect Street

Over four decades in the middle of the nineteenth century, Stephen P. Perkins built or supervised the construction of dozens of buildings in the New Haven area. Born in October, 1807, he was raised on his family's farm in Woodbridge, Connecticut. After a local education, he became apprenticed to builder Horace Butler at the age of 17. He worked for Butler first in New Haven and then in New York, progressing from apprentice to journeyman.

Perkins left Butler's employ in 1832, returned to New Haven, and started his own business as a builder in partnership with John Peck. After nine years, Peck left the firm and Perkins partnered with Harpin Lum for two years. In 1852 he formed the lasting and successful firm of Perkins & Chatfield with his one-time apprentice Philo Chatfield.

For all but thirteen years of his life, Perkins lived on the family farm in Woodbridge where he was born. He was married twice, first in 1832 to Julia Ann Pettit, who died in 1874, and then to Lizzie Williams in 1875. He had two sons, the younger born in 1878 when Perkins was 71.

In civic life, Perkins was an active participant in the early days of the Republican party. He served in the Connecticut Legislature from 1876–77.

Stephen Perkins died suddenly in September 1890 of an apparent heart attack, at the age of 84.

Perkins & Chatfield operated under that name from 1852 to 1875, when Perkins retired. Chatfield added a new partner, George M. Grant, and continued until his own retirement in 1886. The firm was prominently associated with the growth of New Haven, taking construction commissions from mayors, leading businessmen, churches, the hospital, and Yale University.

Perkins & Chatfield built from plans prepared by others, not from their own designs. The firm helped build about 50 significant downtown buildings, many of which remain. These include City Hall in 1861, the Gaius F. Warner House at 1032 Chapel Street designed by Henry Austin in 1860 (shown as built in the old photo, now partially hidden behind the Union League Café), Trinity Church Chapel on George Street, the R.M. Everit house at 641 Whitney Avenue, Yale Senior Societies Skull and Bones (High Street) and Scroll and Key (corner of Wall and College Street), and the first of Yale University's fine arts buildings at 1071 Chapel Street in 1864 (now Street Hall).

The John M. Davies Mansion at 393 Prospect Street is a picturesque Perkins & Chatfield building that has survived a number of ups and downs in its 150-year history. The Davies Mansion was the largest house in New Haven in 1868 when it was built, at 19,000 square feet. Situated at the top of Prospect Street among other notable homes, now all lost, the Davies Mansion came close to demolition in 1980 and was severely damaged by a fire in 1990. It was extensively renovated by Yale University in 2002. Now named Betts House, it is the home of Yale University's Center for the Study of Globalization.

The mansion was built for John M. Davies, co-owner of a shirt manufacturing company. Designed by Henry Austin and David R. Brown, the house is a romantic interpretation of the French Second Empire style. It has an exuberant and irregular profile, with varied roof lines and an off-center tower at the head of a sweeping circular drive. The house was one of eleven properties included in the Historic American Buildings Survey of New Haven. Elizabeth Mills Brown states that it is "one of the few souvenirs that the city can claim of the Gilded Age."

JAMES EDWARD ENGLISH 1812–1890

9 WOOSTER PL

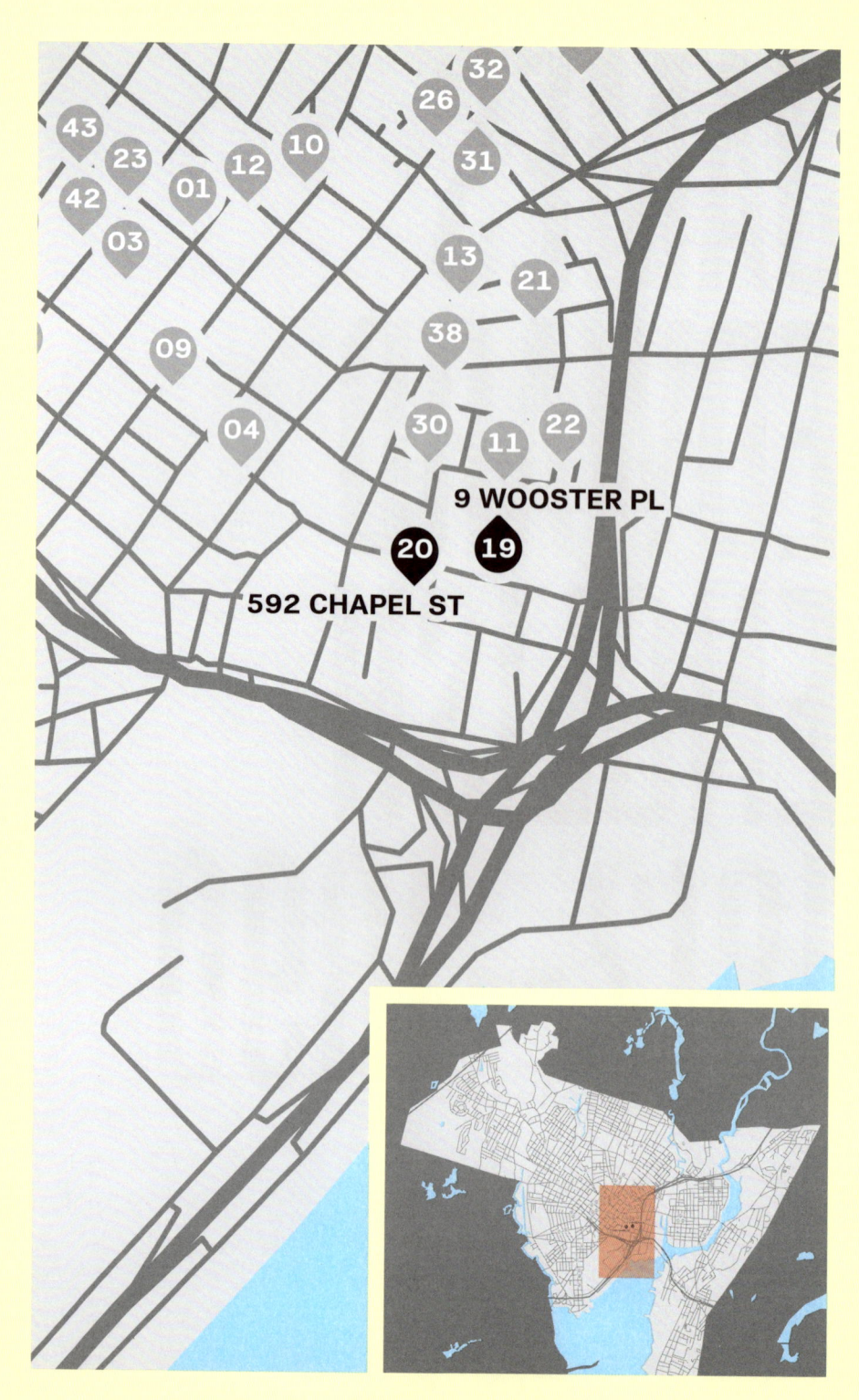

592 CHAPEL ST

74 THE BUILDER BOOK NEW HAVEN PRESERVATION TRUST

19

9 Wooster Place

75 JAMES EDWARD ENGLISH

20

592 Chapel Street

76 THE BUILDER BOOK   NEW HAVEN PRESERVATION TRUST

James Edward English is described in New Haven histories as a politician, serving as Senator and Representative in both the state and national legislatures and as Governor of Connecticut (twice). But before his years in public service, English was trained as a carpenter, a path which gave him a route to commercial and political success.

English was born in March, 1812, in the family home on Chapel Street near York Street. Biographers say he was a self-reliant child, electing (with reluctant parental consent) to live for a time with a farmer in Bethlehem, Connecticut, who had advertised for a live-in farm worker. When he was thirteen, English returned to New Haven for a brief formal education.

In 1828 English was apprenticed to the carpenter Atwater Treat (also included in this book). English was a skilled builder and had a flair for architectural design. When his apprenticeship ended in 1833, he opened a contracting business and for the next three years he built homes to his own designs. With his earnings as a carpenter, he bought a lumberyard, the source of his growing fortune over the next two decades.

English had the energy and capacity to take on more than a dozen investments and civic commitments. With fellow-entrepreneur Hiram Camp, he took over the failing New Haven Clock Company in 1855 and

> "He said that his finest moment in Congress was voting in favor of the Thirteenth Amendment abolishing slavery, despite the opposition of all but a few in his party."

built up one of the largest businesses of its kind in the country. At the outbreak of the Civil War, the New Haven Clock Company employed 300 people and turned out a quarter of a million clocks per year.

English was one of five citizens who put up the initial $300,000 capitalization of the First National Bank of New Haven, opened in 1863. The First National Bank was only the second of its kind in the nation, enabled by Congress to issue paper money with Federal backing. The Bank grew so fast that by 1869, English commissioned a five-story banking house for it at 90 Orange Street (no longer standing).

In 1872, English and four others were named as the first members of the New Haven Harbor Commission, established by the State legislature to improve the facilities of the port.

When the New Haven Hospital outgrew its quarters in the early 1880s, English and two others raised $40,000 for a new building. He was a director of the Connecticut Training School for Nurses and supported the New Haven Orphan Asylum. He gave substantial funds to Yale Law School for the law library and to Yale's Sheffield Scientific School to fund a chair in mathematics. In 1884, English helped to fund the new East Rock Park and the easterly approach was named English Drive by the park commissioners.

English was elected to the New Haven Common Council in the late 1840s, to the Connecticut House of Representatives in 1855, and to the State Senate from 1856–58. He was elected to the U.S. Congress as a Democrat, serving from 1861 to 1865. He said that his finest moment in Congress was voting in favor of the Thirteenth Amendment abolishing slavery, despite the opposition of all but a few in his party. Biographers say he commented to a colleague, "I suppose I am politically ruined, but that day was the happiest of my life."

English served as Governor of Connecticut from 1867 to 1869, lost the 1869 election, but was re-elected for another term in 1870. He went back to Congress in 1872 and in 1875 was appointed to fill out the term of a U.S. Senator who died in office.

English married twice, first to Caroline Fowler, who died in 1874, and then late in life to Anna Robinson Morris, who outlived him. He had four children, only one of whom, Henry, lived to adulthood. English died in March, 1890, and is buried in Evergreen Cemetery. His funeral was a day of mourning across the City, with shops closed along the route of the procession and residents lining the streets.

Although English commissioned many buildings in his lifetime, there may be only one, 9 Wooster Place, remaining today from the three years he worked as a carpenter.

The Rev. Stephen Jewett House at 9 Wooster Place was built in 1833 for Theron Towner, a shipping merchant, who sold it to Jewett. The plans are lost, but Elizabeth Mills Brown speculates that English designed this four-square Italianate villa himself. (The mansard roof and fussy porch were added by others in 1872.) Wooster Square Park was established in 1825, so this and its near-neighbors 37–39 Wooster Place (1833) and 11 Wooster Place (1836) would have been among the first houses to look out on the Park.

English chose New Haven architect Henry Austin to design his own house at 592 Chapel Street in 1845, but very likely did not build it himself since he had moved into the lumber business by then. This is one of the few remaining houses designed by Austin for which the plans exist, housed at Beinecke Rare Book & Manuscript Library. Built as a two-story Italian Villa-style house, the third floor was added after its original construction, giving it an awkward vertical proportion. It has wide overhanging eaves, a band of molding at the original roofline, and exotic fluted porch columns with bulbous bases, sitting on square pedestals.

Other extant buildings commissioned by James English include the brick commercial building at 410–418 State Street, known in the nineteenth century as "English Hall," and the block of row houses at 206–214 Wooster Street, many of which have original cut stone arches and arched transom windows over their entries.

Anna Morris English wrote an "In Memoriam" essay after her husband's death which says, "Governor English, as it were, grew up with his country. He loved the town, and as a poor man… gave it his best energies. As a rich man, he endowed its churches, its hospitals, its university, its schools, and did much to enhance its beauty."

PHILO CHATFIELD
1819–1890

08
14
02
27
29
37
32
26
31
43
23
10
12
01
BATTELL CHAPEL
03
34
13
21
66 LYON ST
15
16
09
38
30
22
11
04
245 GREENE ST
20
19
06
33
40
39
41

66 Lyon Street

245 Greene Street

83 PHILO CHATFIELD

400 College Street / Battell Chapel   23

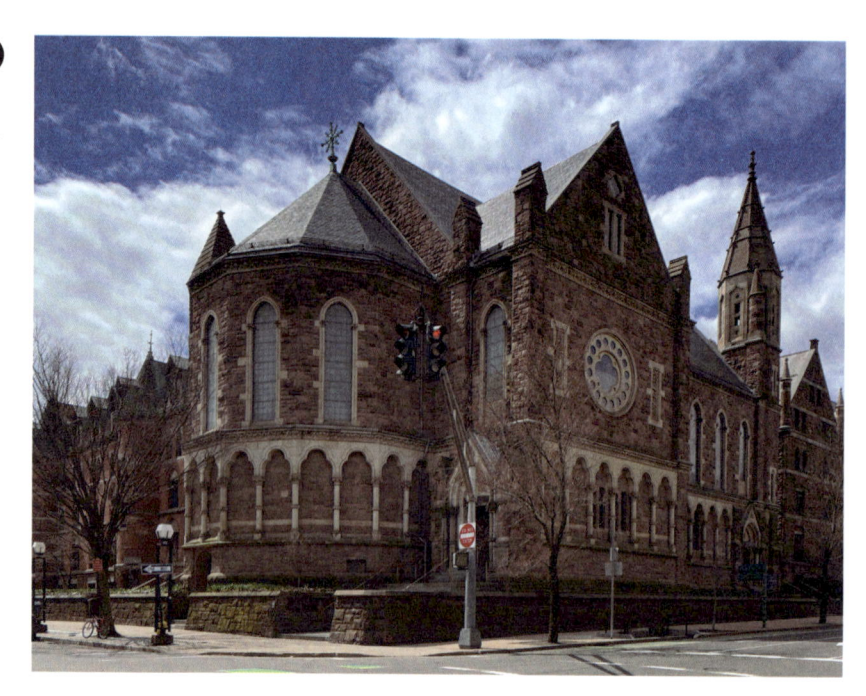

Philo Chatfield worked as a mason in New Haven for over 50 years, partner in a firm that contributed to the stonework of numerous buildings throughout New Haven. Historian Edward Atwater said, "Nearly every street bears evidence of their substantial work."

Chatfield was born in Oxford, Connecticut, in September, 1819, the son of a farmer. He was apprenticed to the mason Stephen Perkins at the age of 17, and by 21 was considered an expert in stone and brick construction. In 1841, Chatfield married Mary E. Lines, with whom he had a daughter, Sarah. When he was 33 years old, in 1852, Chatfield joined Perkins to establish the firm of Perkins & Chatfield.

Like other successful working builders of his era, Chatfield engaged in extensive public service. Many nineteenth-century builders were mentioned in news reports and histories as much for their civic roles as for their construction output. Chatfield was elected to the New Haven Common Council, served a term as Police Commissioner, and was a longtime member of the Board of Public Works. His lasting achievement as a public works commissioner was initiating a plan for East Rock Park and shaping its early development. Authorized by the Connecticut General Assembly in 1880 and designed by landscape architect Donald Grant Mitchell, East Rock Park opened to the public in 1884.

Like other successful working builders of his era, Chatfield engaged in extensive public service. Many nineteenth-century builders were mentioned in news reports and histories as much for their civic roles as for their construction output. Chatfield was elected to the New Haven Common Council, served a term as Police Commissioner, and was a longtime member of the Board of Public Works.

As a prominent businessman, Chatfield was a director of both the Merchants' National Bank and the Connecticut Savings Bank. He was a trustee of the Connecticut State Hospital (now Connecticut Valley Hospital), established in Middletown by the State legislature "to secure suitable care and medical attention" for persons with mental illness.

In 1886 he took on a new partner, George M. Grant, changed the name to Chatfield & Grant, and retired. Philo Chatfield died in March, 1890, and is buried in Evergreen Cemetery.

Chatfield built two houses for himself on Lyon Street. The first, at 69 Lyon, is still standing but much altered. The second, 66 Lyon Street, built in 1858, is a representative example of the Greek Revival style widely adopted by middle class New Haven families in the 1850s and 1860s. A 2½ story frame house (not masonry!), its gable faces the street, defined by long cornice returns and horizontal banding. Elizabeth Mills Brown notes that the return to gable fronts after years of flat-roofed villas marks the beginning of the urge for verticality that characterized the second half of the nineteenth century. The muscular porch of 66 Lyon Street has square columns sitting on square pedestals, topped by a cornice and deep arched friezes.

Despite the trend toward gable roofs, Perkins & Chatfield built a flat-roofed brick house just off Wooster Square, at 245 Greene Street, around 1870. The William Dann House is three bays wide in front, taller than it is wide, but widens at about the mid-point of each side, creating a solid 5-bay block to the rear. A full-width porch with brackets that match the cornice brackets adds detail to the sober brick façade. The Dann House still has its original iron fence, a sophisticated detail common to Wooster Square houses of the time.

Yale University contracted with Perkins & Chatfield to construct a number of buildings including the first Peabody Museum and the first

Divinity Hall and Library, both later removed for a new burst of campus growth. In 1874–76, the firm was the masonry contractor for Battell Chapel, designed by Russell Sturgis, Jr., of New York. A High Victorian Gothic showpiece at the corner of Elm and College Streets, Battell Chapel is Yale's Civil War Memorial. The brownstone exterior is richly decorated with blind arcades, ornamental columns, and a rose window on the Elm Street side, all carved in contrasting sandstone.

In 1870, the Yale campus was a scattered array of buildings on the block bounded by Chapel, High, Elm, and College Streets, including the old Brick Row facing College Street. Over the next three decades, Yale would replace the Brick Row with the enclosed quadrangle that we now know as Old Campus. Together with its neighboring dormitories Farnam Hall and Durfee Hall, built in 1869–71, Battell Chapel firmly established the northeast corner of the quadrangle.

MASSENA CLARK 1811–1890

315 ST. RONAN ST

86 HALLOCK ST

90 THE BUILDER BOOK NEW HAVEN PRESERVATION TRUST

86 Hallock Street

91 MASSENA CLARK

25

315 St. Ronan Street

Massena Cark was a complex character: real estate developer, speculator, entrepreneur, and contract builder. He was viewed by a contemporary biographer as "one of New Haven's foremost citizens, whose long identification with her business interests contributed materially to her progress and development."

Clark was born in 1811 in New York, descended from a family that figured in Connecticut history from early colonial days. His family lived for a time in Stockbridge, Massachusetts and moved to West Haven when Clark was 15. He worked in the Smith & Sherman hardware store for eleven years, until the firm failed in the depression of 1837. Clark had loaned the owner about $3,000, and in return for canceling the debt, he was given a number of carriages and hardware, launching him on his first business venture.

Clark took his carriages to Alabama where he had a brother in the banking business. After his brother died of yellow fever, Clark sold the carriages and began a series of short-term business ventures including managing a "cotton yard." He freed an enslaved man in 1840 and returned with him to New Haven.

Clark married Julia Chatterton and had two sons. He built a store on State Street in 1841, the Massena Clark Block, and carried out a successful import/export business until the Civil War, when the government confiscated his ships for use as military supply ships.

A curious structure traced directly to Massena Clark is the small octagon house at 86 Hallock Street, built in 1877. The eight-sided house sits on a raised brick basement and has a full mansard roof with recessed (not projecting) dormers. Although echoing a stylish model of its era, the Hallock Street octagon is smaller than most, making it a distinctive example.

Then Clark began a 25-year career in speculative real estate, supervising general contractors hired to build more than 300 houses in the New Haven area. From his office at 87 Church Street, he acquired and sold property in New Haven, East Haven, West Haven, North Haven, Hamden and Orange. Clark's real estate offerings appeared in the New Haven press several hundred times in the 1880s. For example, in an advertisement in 1883 in the *Daily Morning Journal and Courier,* Clark offered for sale nine houses in several City neighborhoods, two brick stores (Nos. 96 & 104 State Street), multiple building lots on Whitney, Howard, Dixwell, Kimberly, Greenwich, and Winchester Avenues, and 55 shore lots along Lighthouse Point.

Massena Clark died in 1890 and is buried with his wife in Evergreen Cemetery.

A curious structure traced directly to Massena Clark is the small octagon house at 86 Hallock Street, built in 1877. The eight-sided house sits on a raised brick basement and has a full mansard roof with recessed (not projecting) dormers. Although echoing a stylish model of its era, the Hallock Street octagon is smaller than most, making it a distinctive example.

The octagon house was an exotic building type in the mid-1800s. Orson Fowler, a social reformer, developed the octagon concept and marketed octagon houses as model homes for middle class families, claiming they were more spacious and easier to heat and cool than rectangular-plan structures. Despite his efforts, the rectangular box with gable roof remained a more desirable house type. Built for sale, not for his own use, Clark sold the octagon house a year later to James Hopkins, a coachman.

Clark's own house was a mansion called "Hickory Grove" on the west side of Whitney Avenue opposite Willow Street. Clark hired the firm of Perkins & Chatfield (both men included in this book) to build his imposing house, described at the time as one of the City's finest residences. What remains of Hickory Grove is the stone boundary wall along Whitney Avenue and the large Italianate carriage house at 315 St. Ronan Street, remodeled as a condominium in the 1980s. The picturesque brick carriage house has deeply overhanging eaves supported on scroll-cut brackets.

Massena Clark managed a huge real estate business in the New Haven region in the 1880s with a consistently high reputation. His name appears in newspapers as owner, seller, promoter, and developer in countless transactions, perhaps involving more properties over a 25-year span than any other New Haven business.

WILLIS MINOR SMITH 1819–1896

98   THE BUILDER BOOK   NEW HAVEN PRESERVATION TRUST

26 399 Orange Street

27 77 Prospect Street / Wolf's Head

99 WILLIS MINOR SMITH

28 Soldiers and Sailors Monument, East Rock Park

Willis Minor Smith was born in Woodbridge, Connecticut in 1819, the ninth in a family of ten children. His family is one of the oldest in town, going back to Rev. Woodbridge himself. The family house had a curious history—it contained a secret closet where (many years earlier) two regicides hid when they sought food and shelter. The regicides are historic figures: English judges, William Goffe and Edward Whalley, who hastily departed for the colonies in 1661 to avoid execution for ordering the death of King Charles I. Townspeople in New Haven and Woodbridge, including Willis Smith's great-grandmother, fed the judges and helped them evade officers sent from England to arrest them.

Smith worked on his family's farm until he was 16. He came to New Haven in 1835 and was apprenticed to the masonry firm of Hine, Peck & Perkins. (Stephen Perkins is included in this book.) He served his time as an apprentice and worked as a journeyman mason for six or seven years, some of that time in New York City.

In 1844 Smith married Mary E. Sperry, a descendent of another old Woodbridge family and the sister of Nehemiah Sperry (also included in this book). They had one daughter. Smith formed a construction partnership with Sperry in 1847 which lasted well into the 20th century.

Smith was an active member of the Master Masons Association in New Haven, part of a trade group known as the Builders Exchange. For over

40 years he was an active member of the Third Congregational Society, Church of the Redeemer, in the High Victorian Gothic landmark at 292 Orange Street, built in 1871. Smith died in May, 1896 and is buried in Evergreen Cemetery.

Smith built his own house at 399 Orange Street in 1866, in the fashionable residential area south of Trumbull Street. At the time, it was a fine brick Italianate-style house but was later altered by the addition of a third floor and replacement of the original windows.

The firm of Smith & Sperry built the only surviving structure in New Haven designed by the renowned firm of McKim, Mead & White: the distinctive Wolf's Head clubhouse at 77 Prospect Street, the original home of that Yale University Senior Society. Dedicated in 1884, it stands out from its domestic neighbors with a crusty and forbidding brownstone exterior and stepped Dutch gable roof. The entrance lies behind round arches of decorative stonework and a spiky metal gate. Characteristic of an exclusive student society, the windows are narrow slits recessed into the stone walls. Wolf's Head moved to a new location in 1924 and the building now serves as the home of the University's Institution for Social and Policy Studies.

Willis Smith's greatest achievement was superintending the construction of the Soldiers and Sailors Monument at the top of East Rock. The granite monument was the subject of civic debate, lawsuits, and a botched competition before the designer, Moffit & Doyle, was finally chosen. Smith & Sperry was selected to build the 110-foot tall monument, combining a massive square pedestal, a shaft, and bronze figures. It is dedicated to the men who served in four wars: the Revolutionary War, the War of 1812, the Mexican War, and the Civil War.

The lowest level of the monument is a series of five steps. The top step is four feet wide, to provide a promenade around the pedestal.

Above that is a square base of rough granite about twenty feet high enclosing an interior room and spiral staircase that led to an observation deck near the top. Just above the cornice of this base, bronze statues at the corners represent Prosperity, Victory, History and Patriotism. The slightly tapered shaft rises for 75 feet without interruption except for five louvered openings to light the staircase. At the top, a truncated cone supports the crowning statue, the Angel of Peace.

The monument is significant as an example of nineteenth century idealism on a large scale. The height and statuary were neoclassical forms thought to have an uplifting influence, a statement of the values that society in this era believed a monument should embody.

Construction was carried out in 1886 and 1887, and historian Edward Atwater said "... a more intricate piece of mechanical work was never undertaken in New Haven."

Without benefit of electricity or gasoline engines, Smith devised an adjustable derrick that could be raised and lowered to lay the stones for the shaft of the monument. He perfected a new method for laying stone in below-freezing temperatures and invented a complicated hoist reaching above the monument to enable the workmen to close the opening at the top of the shaft. Unlike falls that commonly occurred in this era from construction work on high, such as church steeples, no fatal accident occurred on this job.

The dedication of the Soldiers and Sailors Monument on June 17, 1887, was the largest celebration in New Haven's history. The bells of Trinity Church rang out at sunrise, answered by gun salutes from a warship in the harbor. Every horse owned by the street railroad was called on to drive carriages to the top of East Rock Park. Along streets hung with flags and bunting, the parade had seven divisions of military and honorary members; two Civil War generals participated. It was reported that 175,000 people attended the parade and ceremony. (The City's population at the time was about 80,000 people.)

Almost half of Willis Smith's 700-word obituary in the *New Haven Daily Morning Journal and Courier* was devoted to this accomplishment. The Soldiers and Sailors Monument is his legacy to the City, visible from miles around.

NEHEMIAH DAY SPERRY
1827–1911

466 ORANGE ST

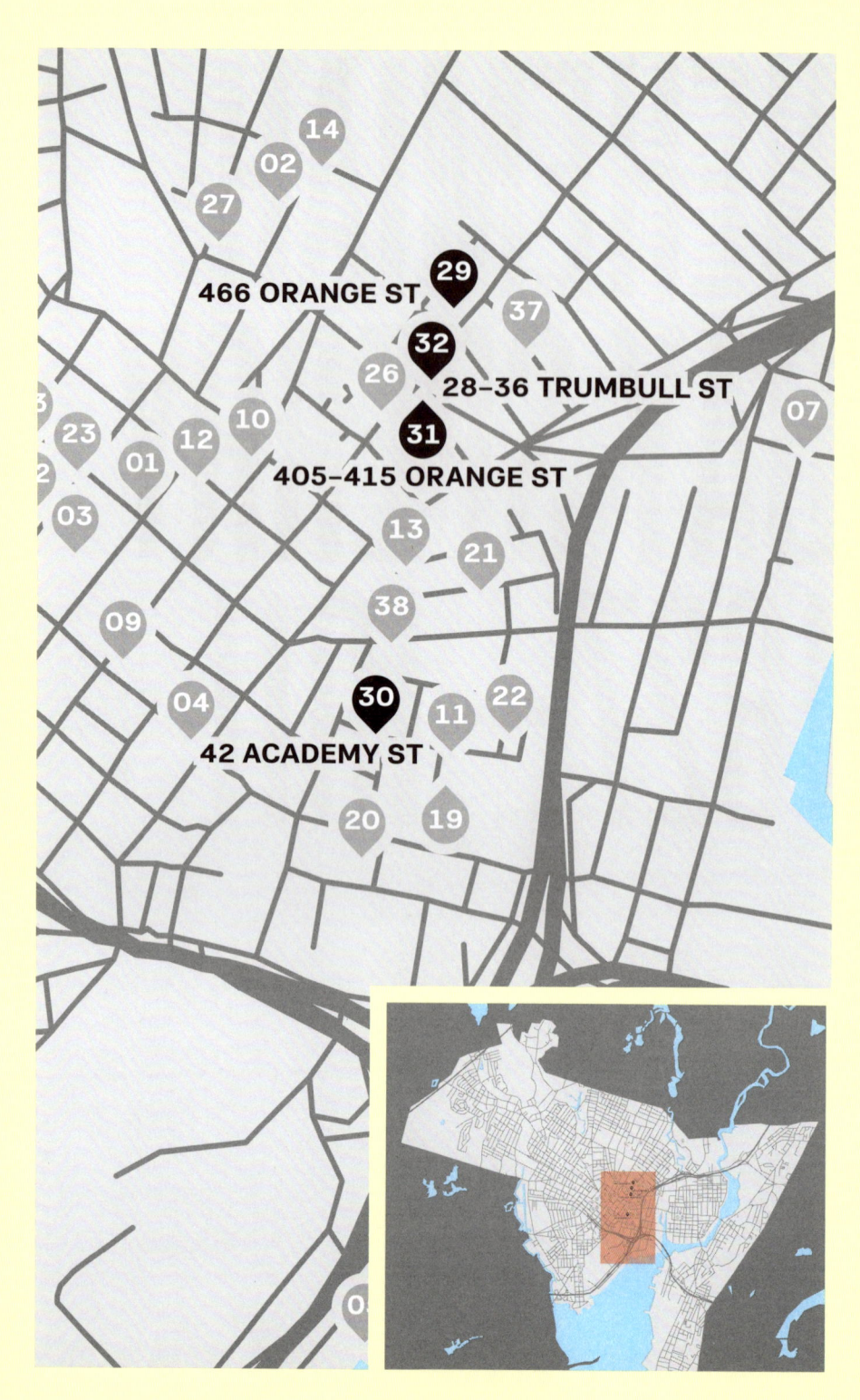

28–36 TRUMBULL ST

405–415 ORANGE ST

42 ACADEMY ST

466 Orange Street

107 NEHEMIAH DAY SPERRY

42 Academy Street

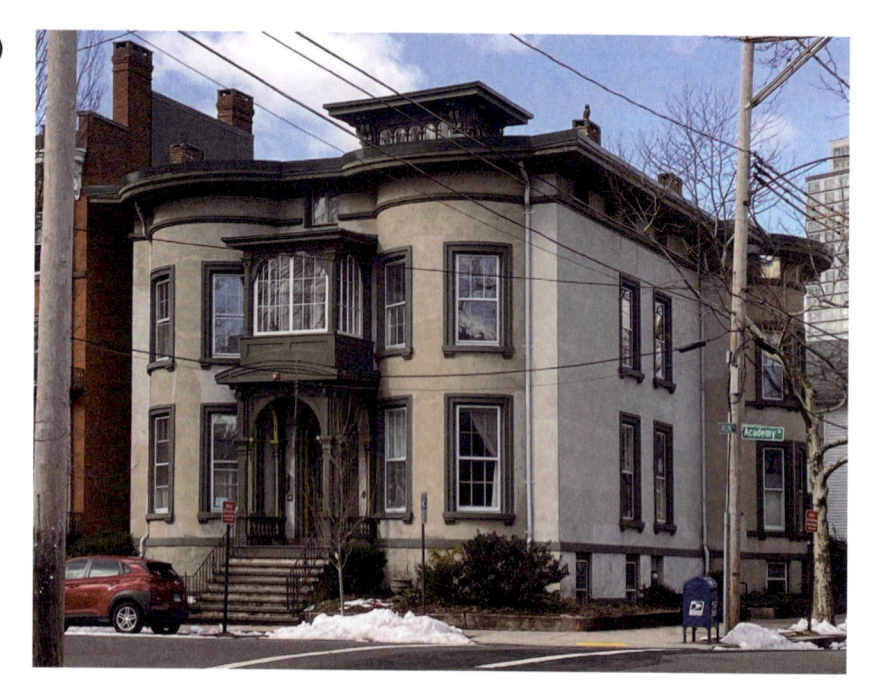

405–415 Orange Street

NEHEMIAH DAY SPERRY

32

28–36 Trumbull Street

Nehemiah Day Sperry was born in 1827 at his family's farm in Woodbridge, CT. He married Eliza H. Sperry (her maiden name) in 1847, with whom he had two daughters. After Eliza died in 1873, he was remarried in 1875 to Minnie B. Newton.

 Educated in a one-room schoolhouse, Sperry graduated from being the school's student to its teacher. His teaching won a regional prize, but he chose a business career. As a young man, Sperry helped establish the New Haven & Derby Railroad, aimed at bringing the trade of the Naugatuck Valley to New Haven. As a separate venture from his career as a mason, Sperry founded a company to construct and operate the Fair Haven and Westville Street Railroad, the first (horse drawn) street car company in Connecticut, and served as its president for ten years.

 Sperry was an early supporter of abolition and chaired the State Republican Committee before and during the Civil War. He was among the Connecticut delegates at the Baltimore convention which nominated Abraham Lincoln to the presidency. Sperry was a New Haven alderman, served two terms as Secretary of the State of Connecticut, and was appointed by President Lincoln as Postmaster General for New Haven, holding the position for six terms (24 years) under seven different Presidents. He remained active in state and

> Sperry was an early supporter of abolition and chaired the State Republican Committee before and during the Civil War. He was among the Connecticut delegates at the Baltimore convention which nominated Abraham Lincoln to the presidency.

national politics and was renowned as a public speaker. From 1895 to 1911, Sperry represented New Haven in the U. S. Congress.

Nehemiah Sperry died in 1911 and is buried in Evergreen Cemetery.

One of the oldest construction firms in New Haven, Smith & Sperry was established in 1846 by Sperry and his brother-in-law, Willis Minor Smith. They took on Arthur Treat as a partner in 1878, changing the name to Smith, Sperry & Treat and later just Sperry & Treat. Sperry's business partners, Willis Smith and Arthur Treat, are included in this book.

Nehemiah Sperry's decades of public service, in addition to his success as a mason, earned glowing mentions in the contemporary press. One biographer described Sperry in 1887 as "tall, erect, dignified, but in disposition...full of kindness, genial, sympathetic, generous, overflowing with fun, and always ready to laugh, even at his own expense."

Sperry's own house at 466 Orange Street was built in 1857, an Italian villa design with a double-bow front. The house has an arched front door and flat-roofed porch with intricate detailing. The bold projecting cornice sits above brackets and a frieze typical of the Italianate style. The Sperry house is contemporary with a number of fashionable large residences on Orange Street from Audubon Street to about Eld Street.

At the same time, Smith & Sperry built a near-twin house at 42 Academy Street, facing Wooster Square, for Edward Rowland, a lumber dealer and railroad official. The Academy Street house boasts a fine monitor and a raised double-height front porch. Its cornice, like the cornice at 466 Orange, is detailed with a heavy band of molding.

Other extant Smith & Sperry buildings include Farnam and Durfee Halls on the Old Campus of Yale University, and row houses at 405–415 Orange Street and 28–36 Trumbull Street. Although rowhouses are not as common in New Haven as in some eastern seaboard cities, the examples on Orange and Trumbull Streets are handsome and well-detailed. The three sets of rowhouses at 405–415 Orange, 28–36 Trumbull Street, plus 40–48 Trumbull Street (see below), combine to form a sophisticated nineteenth century streetscape.

The Orange Street rowhouses are High Victorian Italianate, with a deep cornice on brackets, above dentil molding and a paneled frieze the length of the building. Four stories tall, with generous front steps between small yards, this 1864 structure uses oversized details to give the impression of a single façade. The six matching entries have pedimented hoods resting on large scrolled consoles on each side of double doors. These luxurious details were intended to ensure that buyers viewed the rowhouses as favorably as nearby detached homes. With exceptions due to later modifications, the iron railings at each raised stoop neatly turn the corner and extend along the sidewalk to form a front fence.

Sperry's brother Lucien was also a builder, partnering with Smith & Sperry in several ventures including the row houses at 40–48 Trumbull Street in 1872. Lucien Sperry volunteered with the local militia, known as the Second Company, Governor's Foot Guard, and served as Mayor from 1866 to 1869, although his stature was later diminished when he was convicted of embezzlement.

Unlike contractors who built by hand and did not survive twentieth century construction innovations, Nehemiah Sperry's company adapted and remained in business for almost 90 years. Under the name of the Sperry & Treat Co., the firm built many buildings on the Yale University campus, including the residential college shown in the picture at the front of this book. The Sperry & Treat Co. was also hired by Yale University to build both the Sterling Law School complex in 1929 and the Divinity School campus on upper Prospect Street in 1931. The firm last appears in a City Directory in 1941.

ARTHUR BARNES TREAT
1853 – 1913

37 HIGH ST

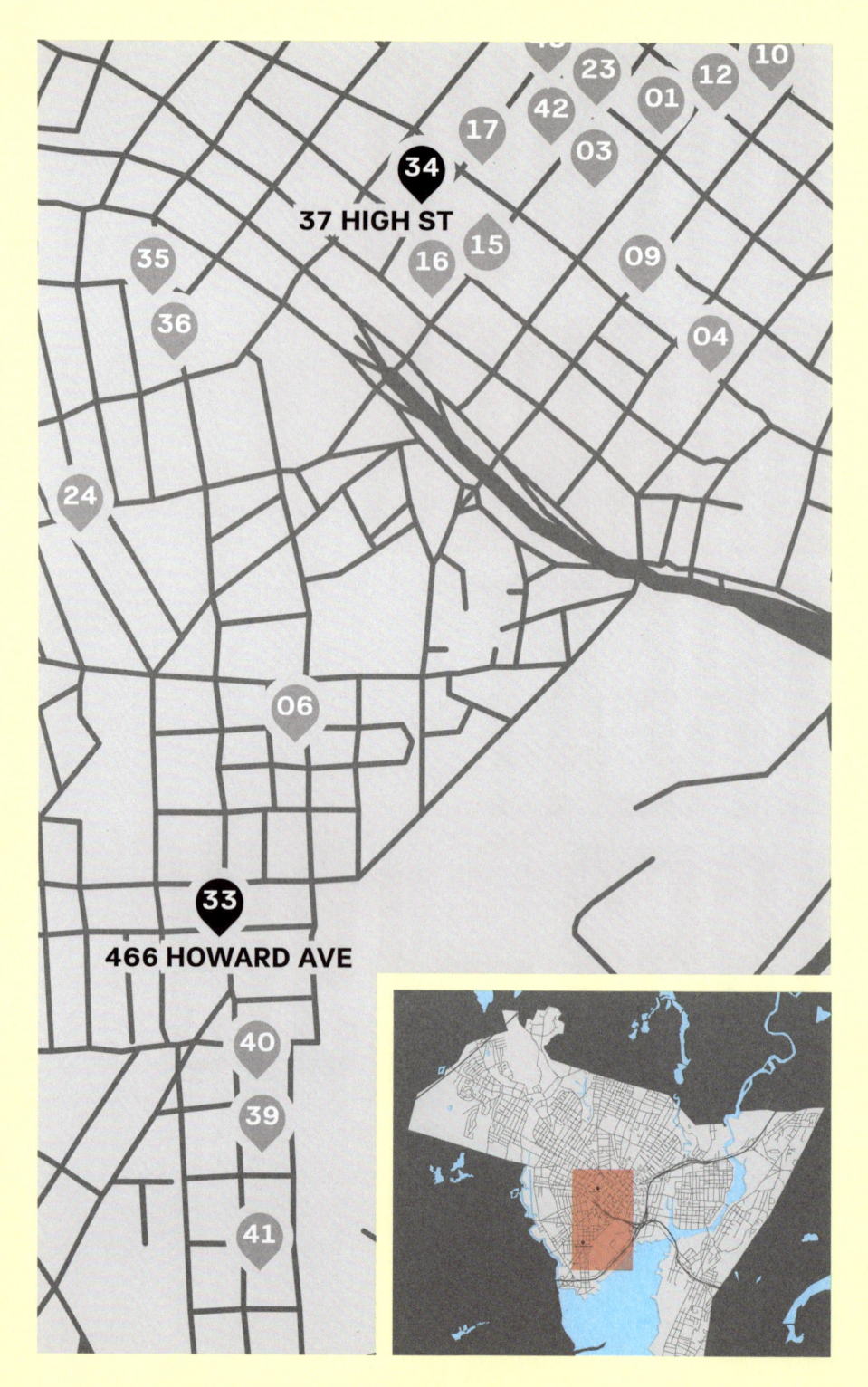

466 HOWARD AVE

466 Howard Avenue

ARTHUR BARNES TREAT

34

37 High Street

Arthur Barnes Treat was descended from early Connecticut settlers, beginning with Richard Treat who came to the American colonies in 1638. Arthur Treat was a prominent builder and contractor, one of many masons associated with the firm of Smith & Sperry.

Treat was born on the family's 200-acre farm in Orange, Connecticut in 1853. At the age of fourteen, he secured his first business contract to supply the Derby Railroad Company with stone. After his education in Orange, Treat attended Oberlin College in Ohio for a year. In 1870, he returned to New Haven as an apprentice and journeyman at Smith & Sperry for eight years.

He married Leona Weeks in 1876. They had three children who lived to adulthood and a fourth child who died in infancy. Treat later remarried twice, first to Catherine Stanley and then to Esther Lamport, and had two more children.

Treat was a trustee of the Howard Avenue Congregational Church, sang in the church choir as a solo tenor, and directed another choral society for many years. He was a member of the Sons of the Revolution, honoring his great-grandfather who fought at Valley Forge, and belonged to the Second Company, Governor's Foot Guard, ending his service with the rank of captain. In his later years, Treat lived on his farm in Orange. He died in December, 1913, from what was judged to be indigestion, and is buried in Evergreen Cemetery.

Arthur Treat's house at 466 Howard Avenue is a showpiece of skillful brickwork in the Queen Anne style. Built in 1882, the house has a two-story porch with highly stylized columns. Similar in size and shape to other gable-front houses, it is distinguished by bands of molded and paneled brick, including a panel of textured brick under the peak of the gable.

In 1878 Treat left Smith & Sperry and formed his own firm with Hillard Fenn, also a former Smith & Sperry apprentice. Fenn died soon after, so Treat rejoined Smith & Sperry as a partner, making the firm Smith, Sperry & Treat, later just Sperry & Treat. He had a supervisory role in the construction of at least 34 Yale University buildings, including Old Campus dormitories which still stand. Often called the "college builders" in newspapers of the day, the firm worked for ten different architects on the Yale projects and employed about 125 men.

After his partner, Nehemiah Sperry (included in this book), was elected to Congress and worked most of the year in Washington, D. C., Treat was effectively the manager of the firm. He also worked in other locales and established a separate firm, A. B. Treat & Co., in 1885 to handle contracts in Bridgeport, Connecticut.

Arthur Treat's house at 466 Howard Avenue is a showpiece of skillful brickwork in the Queen Anne style. Built in 1882, the house has a two-story porch with highly stylized columns. Similar in size and shape to other gable-front houses, it is distinguished by bands of molded and paneled brick, including a panel of textured brick under the peak of the gable. Windows on the façade have arched brick headers and the triple attic windows are capped with semi-circular brick arches in a sunburst motif, illustrating the mason's craftsmanship.

Treat built an elegant Queen Anne dwelling at 37 High Street in 1882 for George C. Pettis, a local manufacturer. In another display of skilled brickwork, the windows have two-tone arched headers with keystones. Brick stringcourses of molded scrolls and quatrefoils delineate each floor. The attic has a 4-part window and a triangular panel under the peak of the gable, inlaid with a geometric design. A clean-lined porch with slim columns supporting a pediment hood shelters a double-door entry. The property retains its pineapple-topped stone driveway pillars and a fragment of its original iron fence.

Arthur Treat is associated with New Haven's tremendous growth in the second half of the nineteenth century, most of his buildings now replaced with later construction. He was known for reliable construction of buildings in all parts of the City and had a high reputation as a businessman of "indomitable will and untiring energy," according to historian Edward Atwater.

LYMAN V. TREAT 1821–1896 & GEORGE M. TREAT 1856–1910

840 HOWARD AVE
836 HOWARD AVE

35 | 840 Howard Avenue

125 LYMAN V. TREAT & GEORGE M. TREAT

36

836 Howard Avenue

Lyman and George Treat were father and son masons in New Haven, principals in the firm of L.V. Treat & Sons. Lyman was born in May, 1821, and married Susan Merwin. They had two sons, Frank and George, who was born in 1856. Little is known about Frank Treat's life.

At the time of the 1870 Census, the family lived at 78 Ward Street. Both sons joined their father as masons, and in 1874 the family moved to the brick house Lyman built at 840 Howard Avenue (at the time, 500 Howard), which also held the offices of the masonry business.

Lyman Treat died in October, 1896, and is buried in Evergreen Cemetery.

George Treat married Nellie E. Disbrow in 1885 and a year later built his own house at 836 Howard Avenue (then 498 Howard), next door to his father's house. George and Nellie had two children, a boy and a girl. George prospered and owned properties on Davenport and Dixwell Avenues and on Meadow and Commerce Streets, but he developed physical and mental health issues and became unable to manage his affairs. Nellie divorced him in 1898 and George was placed under the conservatorship of his brother Frank a year later.

Although the probate court dismissed and then reinstated the conservatorship over several years, George was eventually committed to a mental health facility in 1904. He died in October, 1910.

The homes the Treats built for themselves were showpieces of masonry skill, incorporating an array of brickwork details. The two houses illustrate the change in fashionable architectural styles from the 1870s to the 1880s.

Lyman's house, more than a decade earlier than George's, is a three-story brick Victorian with Renaissance Revival details such as stone window headers of alternating shapes and bold string courses of angled soldier-course bricks between the floors. The shallow roof gable is parallel to the street, allowing for decorative eave trim and a row of shapely brackets.

George's house is a distinct example of the Queen Anne style, with ornate porch trim and a steep gable facing the street. The façade features large arched multi-pane windows with rich brick trim, decorative brickwork below the attic and corbeling above the second floor, stained glass windows, terra cotta tiles inset at street level, and other showy details.

While incorporating lively personal choices, the styles of these two houses are representative of nineteenth century buildings seen throughout New Haven.

GEORGE PLATT MERWIN 1828–1905

22 ELD ST

938 GRAND AVE

130   THE BUILDER BOOK   NEW HAVEN PRESERVATION TRUST

22 Eld Street

131   GEORGE PLATT MERWIN

38

938 Grand Avenue (135–139 Olive Street)

132　THE BUILDER BOOK　NEW HAVEN PRESERVATION TRUST

George Platt Merwin's ancestors came from Wales and farmed in Milford for three generations. Merwin was born in 1828 and spent his early life on the farm. He moved to New Haven when he was 18 to learn the carpentry trade. After several years as a journeyman, he formed a building company with two partners, later buying them out and joining forces with William R. Hubbell. For 38 years, Hubbell & Merwin was one of the City's best-known contractors, building frame houses on Edwards, Cottage, Stanley, Canner, Lawrence, and Ferry Streets, among others.

Merwin married Laura Whiting in 1856 and had two sons and a daughter. He was a New Haven Councilman for two years and chaired the committee overseeing the fire department. Merwin was instrumental in acquiring the first steam-powered fire engine in the year that New Haven changed its fire-fighting equipment from hand pumps to steam.

After Hubbell's death, Merwin continued alone until 1896 and then took his two sons into the firm. As late as 1904, Merwin is still listed in the City Directory as president and treasurer of his firm. He died in May, 1905, at the age of 76 and is buried in Evergreen Cemetery.

Hubbell & Merwin employed as many as 30 people and operated their own mill, fabricating moldings, decorative woodwork, sashes and doors for their projects. The development of mass-produced millwork in the mid-nineteenth century reinforced the popular taste for elaboration and made Victorian gingerbread affordable to middle class homebuyers. Off-site manufacturing allowed the firm to finish projects faster and take on more contracts.

An example of Merwin's work is the well-preserved house at 22 Eld Street, built in 1857 in the mixture of Greek Revival and Italianate styles common in New Haven in the 1850s. Merwin purchased the undeveloped lot for $300, built his house, and lived there for the remainder of his life. The house has a side-hall plan, with a gable roof facing the street. Façade windows have bold headers and (most likely) their original 6-pane upper sashes. The elegant front porch is dressed up with fluted Ionic columns and a cornice supported by brackets.

The firm also built commercial structures, including an extension of the Greek Revival building at the corner of Grand Avenue and Olive Street known as the Atwater Block. The original square 2½ story brick structure facing Grand Avenue was built about 1835 by William Atwater. Around the time the building was sold in 1854, Hubbell & Merwin built a 56' long addition in the same style, facing Olive Street. A storefront was added in the mid-20th century.

The Atwater Block is a rare example of a pre-Civil War multi-tenant building, either residential or commercial. Modeled on a restrained style seen in the earlier Exchange Building (described in this book), its ornament consists primarily of stone lintels and sills. The blocky form, rows of regularly-spaced windows and lean cornice signified a functional approach that became more common as the City's commercial importance grew.

GEORGE A. BALDWIN 1830–1903

333 HOWARD AVE

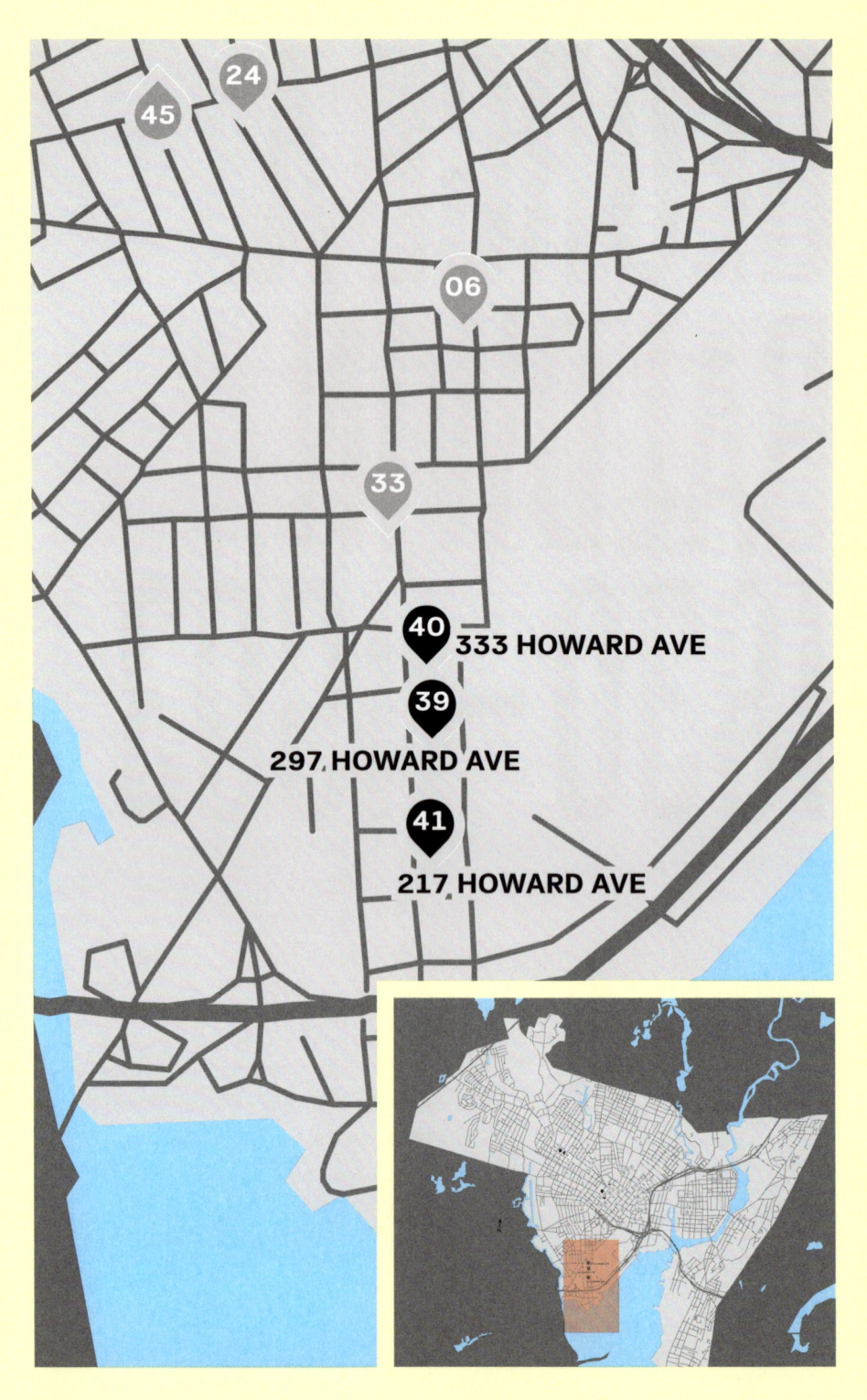

297 HOWARD AVE

217 HOWARD AVE

136   THE BUILDER BOOK   NEW HAVEN PRESERVATION TRUST

39 297 Howard Avenue

40 333 Howard Avenue

137　GEORGE A. BALDWIN

41

217 Howard Avenue

George A. Baldwin was born in 1830 in Oxford, Connecticut, and came to New Haven as a young man to learn the masonry trade. He married Mary Catlin in 1851 and they had two sons and two daughters. The Baldwins first lived at what was then No. 23 White Street and later lived at 57 Lafayette Street, both residences doubling as Baldwin's business office.

When he was about 30 years old, Baldwin joined the sixteen men appointed as the "Night Watch," the precursor of the City's police force. At the end of the Civil War, he resigned from the Night Watch and opened a masonry business. By 1880, both sons, Harry and George E., had joined G.A. Baldwin & Sons; Harry eventually became a full partner. The firm bid on and received masonry contracts for a number of public schools including the Gregory Street School, Washington School and Webster School, none of them extant today. In 1888, Baldwin built a house for his family at 297 Howard Avenue, described below.

He was active in Fourth Ward politics, serving as a registrar of voters and a member of the Ward Committee. He was nominated (but not elected) to the City Council in 1888. Baldwin was a respected member of the New Haven Commandery No. 2, Knights Templar, and a member of the Trumbull Lodge, Franklin Chapter, of the Free Masons.

Baldwin's most imposing work is 217 Howard Avenue, built in 1887 for his son George E. Baldwin. The Historic Resources Inventory (HRI) calls this one of the finest houses in City Point, a Queen Anne structure with the variety of textures and decorative elements characteristic of that style.

Baldwin died September 16, 1903, at 74, from complications of diabetes, and is buried in Evergreen Cemetery. News reports state that more than 100 Knights Templar attended his funeral, led by the Second Regiment Band.

Baldwin's house at 297 Howard Avenue is a fine example of polychrome Queen Anne-style brickwork, built in 1888. A 2½ story house with a cross-gable roof, it has two belt courses of yellow and black bricks across the front, extending around both east and west facades. The windows are capped by segmental arches of yellow and black brick, a lively individual touch. Two small windows over the entry have been bricked in but their surrounds are still visible.

The easterly gable sits above a generous three-sided bay with bi-colored brick trim.

In the same year, Baldwin built a similar cross-gable house at 333 Howard Avenue for his son Harry. This house repeats the motifs of yellow brick belt courses and segmental arches above the windows, but retains all three second story windows and the original three-part attic window, each with an arched header. The straightforward arrangement of windows gives dignity to the façade. The elegant art glass window in the stair hall is a reminder of the stature of Howard Avenue in the 1880s. The First Street side, filled with a dozen more windows with arched headers, is surprisingly deep, approximately double the width of the Howard Avenue façade, and has more ornamental brickwork above the bay and in the peak of the gable.

Baldwin's most imposing work is 217 Howard Avenue, built in 1887 for his son George E. Baldwin. The Historic Resources Inventory (HRI) calls this one of the finest houses in City Point, a Queen Anne structure with the variety of textures and decorative elements characteristic of that style. The HRI describes it as a "complicated" façade with pediments over the first and second story porches and the window facing Howard

Avenue. It has both a hipped and gabled roof, with brackets under the eaves. The façade steps back from the street, creating a small square porch in the cut-out corner. The house incorporates a heady mix of materials: the gables are covered with intricate clapboard panels, the second floor bay facing Howard is sheathed in overlapping shingles; and the body of the house is brick. Although linked to 297 and 333 Howard by family connections, this house takes greater joy in combining an array of elaborate features.

With three substantial houses in the Howard Avenue blocks between First and Fourth Streets, the impact of G. A. Baldwin & Sons on this neighborhood is both solid and fanciful, even 130 years later.

CHARLES M. McLINN
1833–1906

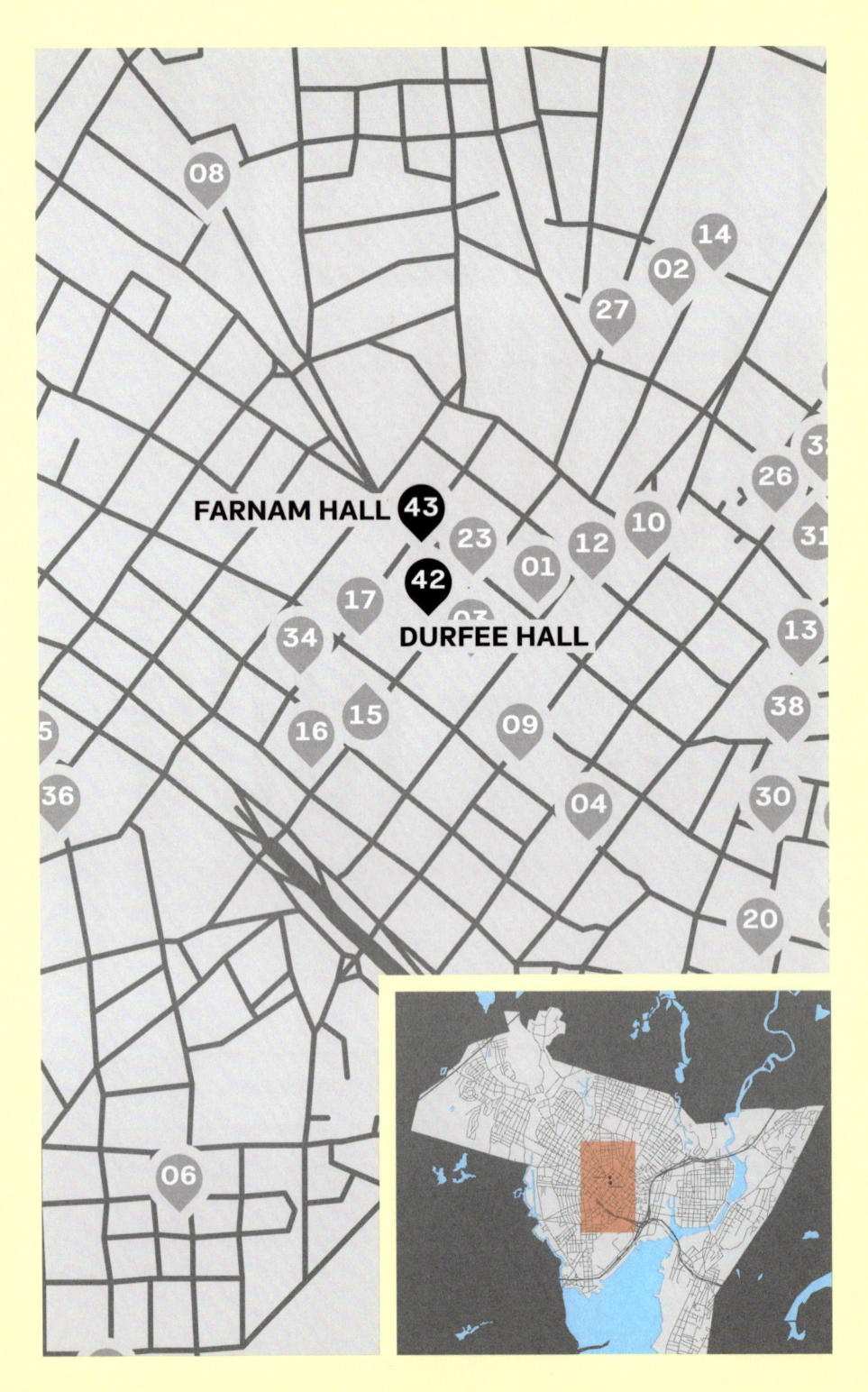

144 THE BUILDER BOOK   NEW HAVEN PRESERVATION TRUST

380 College Street / Farnam Hall

145   CHARLES M. MCLINN

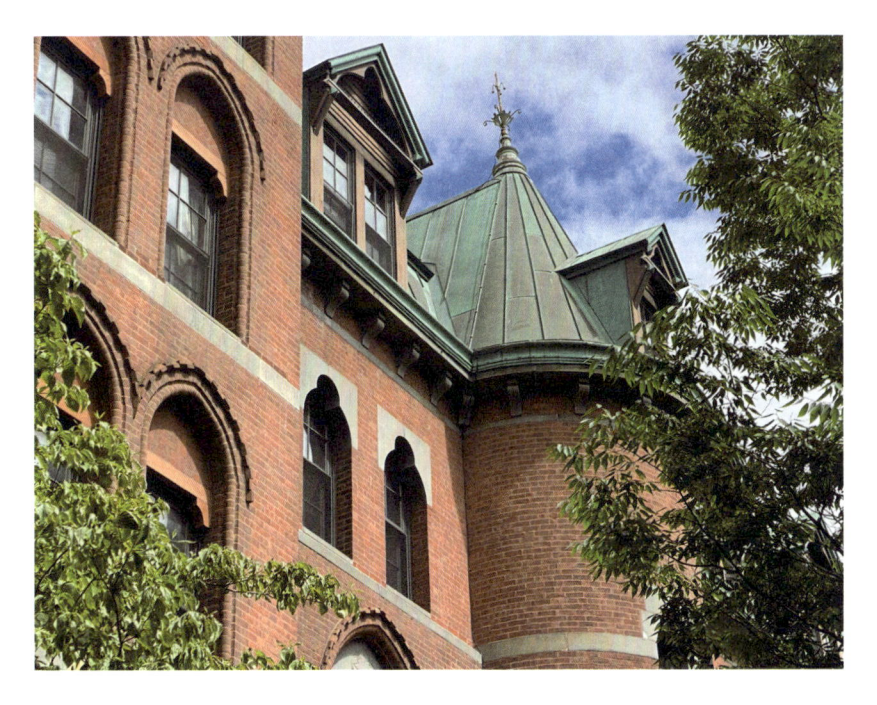

43 — 198 Elm Street / Durfee Hall

Charles M. McLinn began full-time work as the head carpenter at Yale University in 1870 and was employed by the University to improve and maintain its expanding campus for 36 years, operating from a University workshop on High Street.

Born in 1833, McLinn learned the carpentry trade from William Hancock, a well-respected free Black contractor in New Bern, North Carolina. In 1852, Hancock, McLinn and other Blacks left North Carolina and moved to New Haven. McLinn began his New Haven career working for Atwater Treat (also included in this book), who built a number of notable downtown buildings along with some Yale buildings no longer standing.

As a trustee and leading member of the Temple Street Congregational Church, McLinn specialized in business matters such as the care of the building and church finances. He was a leader in moving the congregation to the new Congregational Church at 100 Dixwell Avenue in 1886, where he served as trustee and church clerk. His name appears on many financial and estate planning documents, witnessing wills and managing family funds.

McLinn married Ellen A. Skinner in 1855 and they had six children, two of whom died young. The McLinn family home was at 10–12 Edgewood Avenue, built around 1865 and part of a distinctive cluster of mid-19th century houses at the eastern end of Edgewood Avenue.

In 1884, McLinn was appointed an honorary commissioner to promote Connecticut's role in the World's Industrial Fair in New Orleans. He led a state-wide effort to secure exhibits from the Black community and personally paid for shipping exhibit materials to the exhibition site.

McLinn's work at Yale and his church leadership gave him prominence in New Haven's expanding Black community. He was the first Black member of the New Haven City Council, elected in 1874. McLinn was active in the Republican Party and served as a vice president of the Republican Town Committee in 1891 and 1892.

In 1891, McLinn was appointed to a committee charged with adding a training school "in the mechanical arts" for young Blacks at the Goffe Street School, located at Goffe and Sperry Streets.

Charles McLinn died on November 30, 1906, and is buried in Evergreen Cemetery. At his funeral, he was remembered by citizens across the City and Yale officers and faculty, including former Yale President Timothy Dwight V and Yale President Arthur Twining Hadley.

McLinn worked during the period of greatest growth of Yale's Old Campus, bounded by College, Chapel, High and Elm Streets. Old Campus buildings built between 1870 and 1900 include Farnam Hall, Durfee Hall, Lawrance Hall, Welch Hall, Phelps Hall and archway, and Battell Chapel. McLinn also had a long-standing assignment to care for President Dwight's large and fashionable house at 126 College Street (later 470 College), demolished in 1916.

GEORGE BOHN 1848–1915

21 KOSSUTH ST

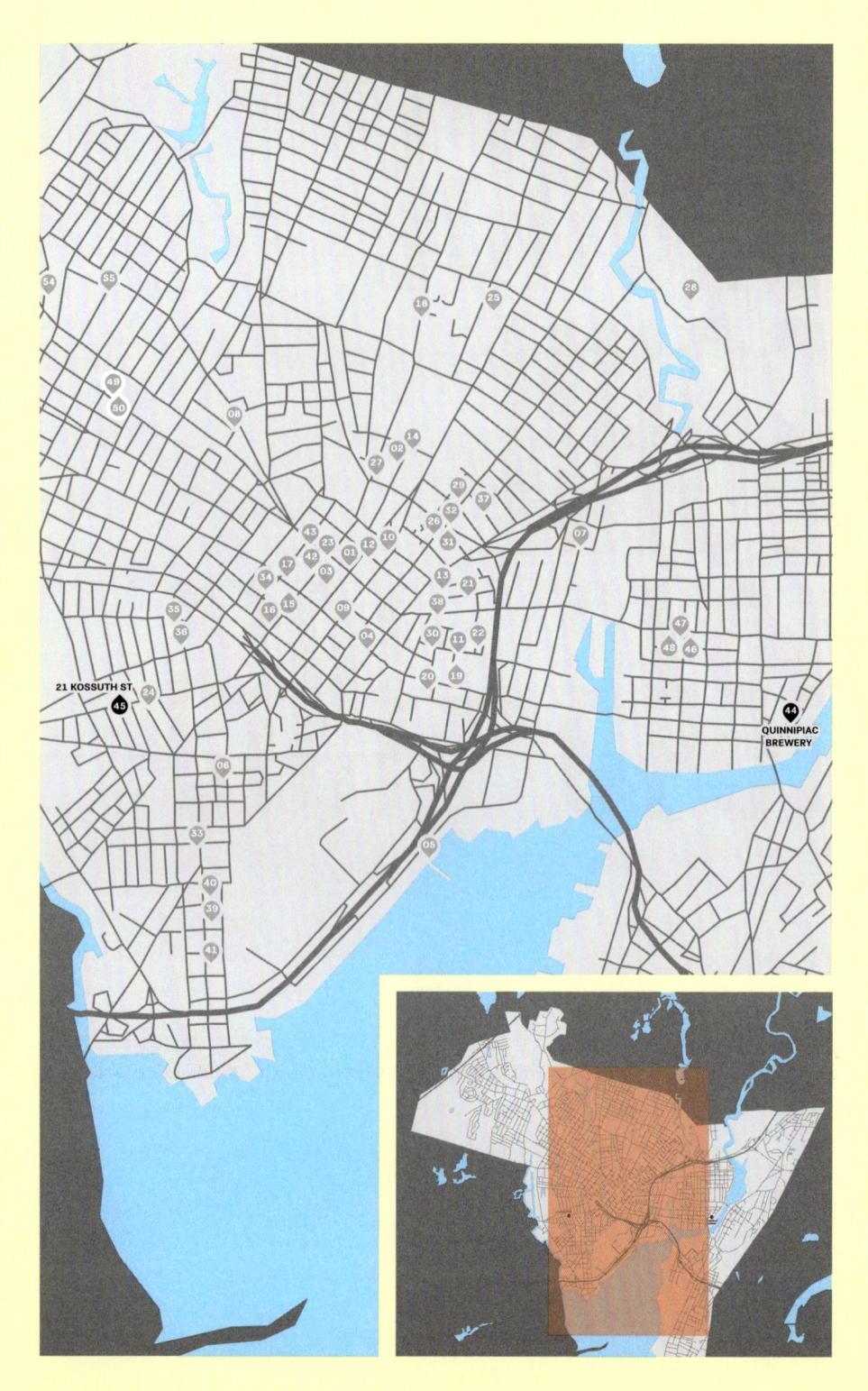

QUINNIPIAC BREWERY

150   THE BUILDER BOOK   NEW HAVEN PRESERVATION TRUST

44　21 River Street / Quinnipiac Brewery

151　GEORGE BOHN

21 Kossuth Street

George Bohn was born in 1848 in Alsace, France. In August of 1870, he joined the French army when France invaded Germany at the start of the Franco-Prussian War. A series of swift German victories in eastern France, culminating in the siege of Metz, saw Emperor Napoleon III decisively defeated. Bohn was captured at Metz and spent seven months in a military prison.

Once released, he came to the United States in 1871 with his wife Margaret and settled in New Haven, where they had four sons and three daughters. Bohn was naturalized as a citizen in 1874. He became active in local politics and served on Democratic ward committees from the Third Ward for two decades.

Bohn established a masonry business and appears to have been a sole proprietor, employing members of his family. His brothers, Dominick and Michael Bohn, and nephew, Henry Bohn, immigrated from France in 1879 and joined George in New Haven. Later his son joined the firm. George Bohn died in 1915 and is buried in St. Lawrence Cemetery, West Haven.

The Bohn firm built a series of two-story houses around Columbus Avenue, West Street, and Congress Avenue. In 1895, Bohn built a house for his family at 21 Kossuth Street, made of buff brick with two flats. A townhouse style unusual in this neighborhood, the house may

George Bohn was born in 1848 in Alsace, France. In August of 1870, he joined the French army when France invaded Germany at the start of the Franco-Prussian War. A series of swift German victories in eastern France, culminating in the siege of Metz, saw Emperor Napoleon III decisively defeated. Bohn was captured at Metz and spent seven months in a military prison.

reflect the growth in urban density near the turn of the 20th century. The shallow gable is perpendicular to the street, giving the impression of a flat roof. Five oversized windows on the façade have headers of segmented brick arches trimmed with precise "nail-head" caps. According to City Directories, Bohn's son Joseph lived in the second flat.

In 1885 the Quinnipiac Brewery at the intersection of Ferry, River, and East Pearl Streets in Fair Haven burned to the ground. It was rebuilt quickly and by the early 1890s sold its product throughout New England. In 1896, Bohn's firm was hired to build a six-story addition to the brewhouse, designed by Leoni Robinson to give the brewery a formal façade, with three blind arches above the huge rail entrance and textural effects including brownstone banding and rough-hewn corner quoins, brick dentils outlining the window heads, and multi-layered corbels under the cornice. Although seemingly a false front, filling in a triangular space between the wall of the earlier brew house and the line of River Street, the addition had functional purposes as well: it housed an elevator, a stairway to the upper floors, and a bucket conveyor for raising grain to the top stories. These improvements reportedly used 150 tons of iron to hold the new 350-barrel capacity brewing tank.

Sadly, Bohn's brother Dominick died on this jobsite after falling from the scaffolding.

Bohn also built a barn and a three-story brick addition to the rear of the brewhouse, likely used for cold storage. This wing had thick stucco walls built of hollow-core thermal brick over a basement with a brick-vaulted ceiling resting on a series of brick arches.

The Quinnipiac Brewery embodied the transition of beer production from smaller local breweries to those producing it on a more industrial scale, with larger equipment and integral support facilities made possible by advances in refrigeration. Because most of his work was limited to two or three stories, Bohn might have been an odd choice for a job of this height and scope, but the result is a convincing demonstration of masonry skill.

THOMAS F. LOWE 1851–1888

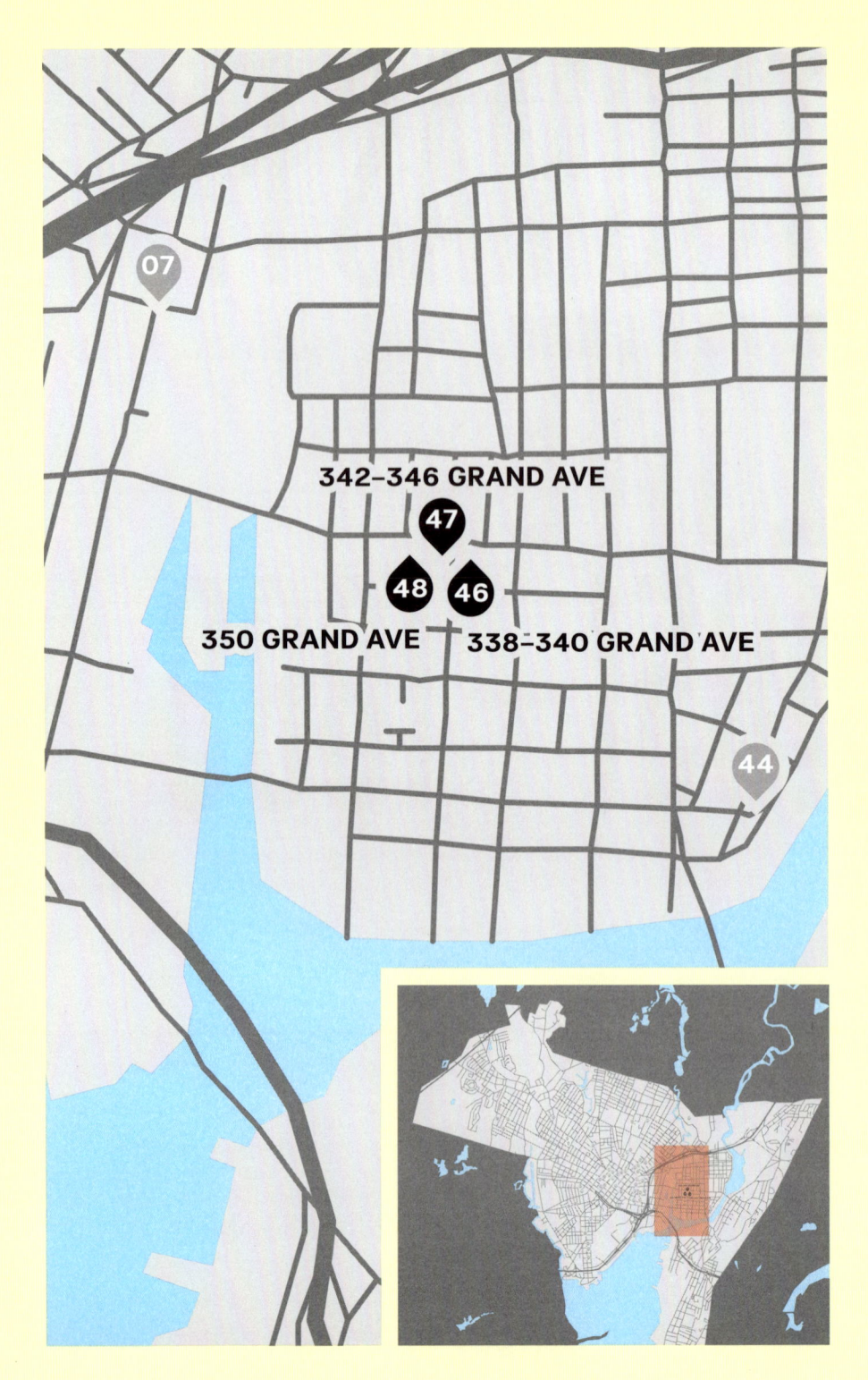

342–346 GRAND AVE
47
48 46
350 GRAND AVE   338–340 GRAND AVE

158   THE BUILDER BOOK   NEW HAVEN PRESERVATION TRUST

338–340 Grand Avenue

159 THOMAS F. LOWE

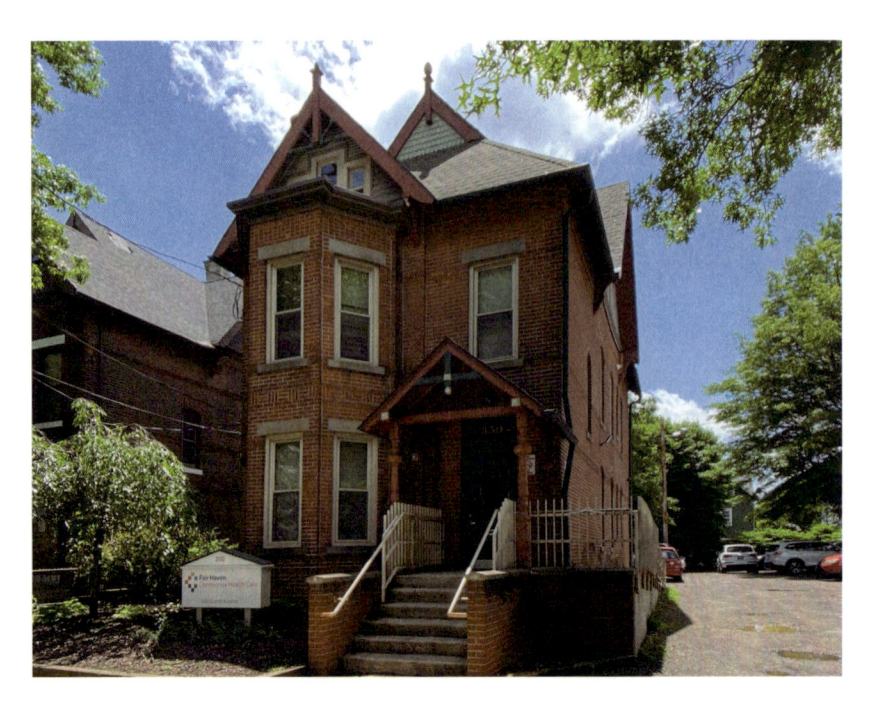

47 342–346 Grand Avenue

48 350 Grand Avenue

160   THE BUILDER BOOK   NEW HAVEN PRESERVATION TRUST

Born in Ireland in 1851, Thomas Lowe was described by a biographer in 1887 as "a self-made man, who with work as his watchword and honesty as his guide, has been quick to see and ready to grasp his opportunities." Despite what seemed to be a promising future, Lowe died at the age of 36, the year after this praise was written, leaving his wife, Anna, and two young children.

After Lowe immigrated to Connecticut, he was trained in carpentry in Waterbury and employed in Bridgeport before moving to New Haven in 1872. He and his family first lived at 141 Exchange Street and later moved to one of his Grand Avenue houses.

He opened his business in 1874 and it immediately flourished. Lowe's shop at 229 Lloyd Street eventually employed more than twenty workers. He purchased a number of lots in central New Haven and in Fair Haven, especially on Lloyd, James, Woolsey and Exchange Streets, which he developed and resold. By the time he died, he had become a prodigious contractor, known for combining elegance and comfort across dozens of buildings.

Thomas Lowe's commercial buildings, including a renovated store for the Edward Malley Co. and carriage-factory buildings on Wooster Street, no longer exist. Today, we know Lowe from a cluster of five brick houses anchoring two blocks of Grand Avenue. Curiously, his legacy is in masonry, not carpentry, suggesting the range of skills among his workmen.

Situated in a dense residential and commercial district, the brick double house at 338–340 Grand was built in 1885. Each side was sold to a member of the Bishop family for $3,000. It is a wide Queen Anne-style structure with most of its original features intact. The double porch with turned columns is symmetrically framed by ten tall windows. Two gables trimmed with fish-scale shingles face the street, one on each side of a central dormer. Matching two-story bay window projections give added dimension to the side facades. After Lowe's death in 1888, his wife Anna lived in this house until she died in 1906.

Lowe built three brick Queen Anne-style houses just to the west at 342, 346, and 350 Grand Avenue in 1886. Together with 338-340, the buildings form a striking line of masonry and carpentry flourishes. The proportions of 342, 346, and 350 are similar, but the detailing— irregular gables and roof lines, "stickwork" eave trim, and bay windows— is varied so no two are identical. The corner treatment of number 342, at the intersection of Grand Avenue and Lloyd Street, is unusual and effective. The angled bay has four windows under a semi-circular colored-glass window surrounded by a brickwork arch, all topped by an ornate gable.

These five imposing houses are a reminder of the prosperous residential history of Grand Avenue.

ETTORE FRATTARI
c.1867–1954

748–752 ELM ST
49
50
742 ELM ST

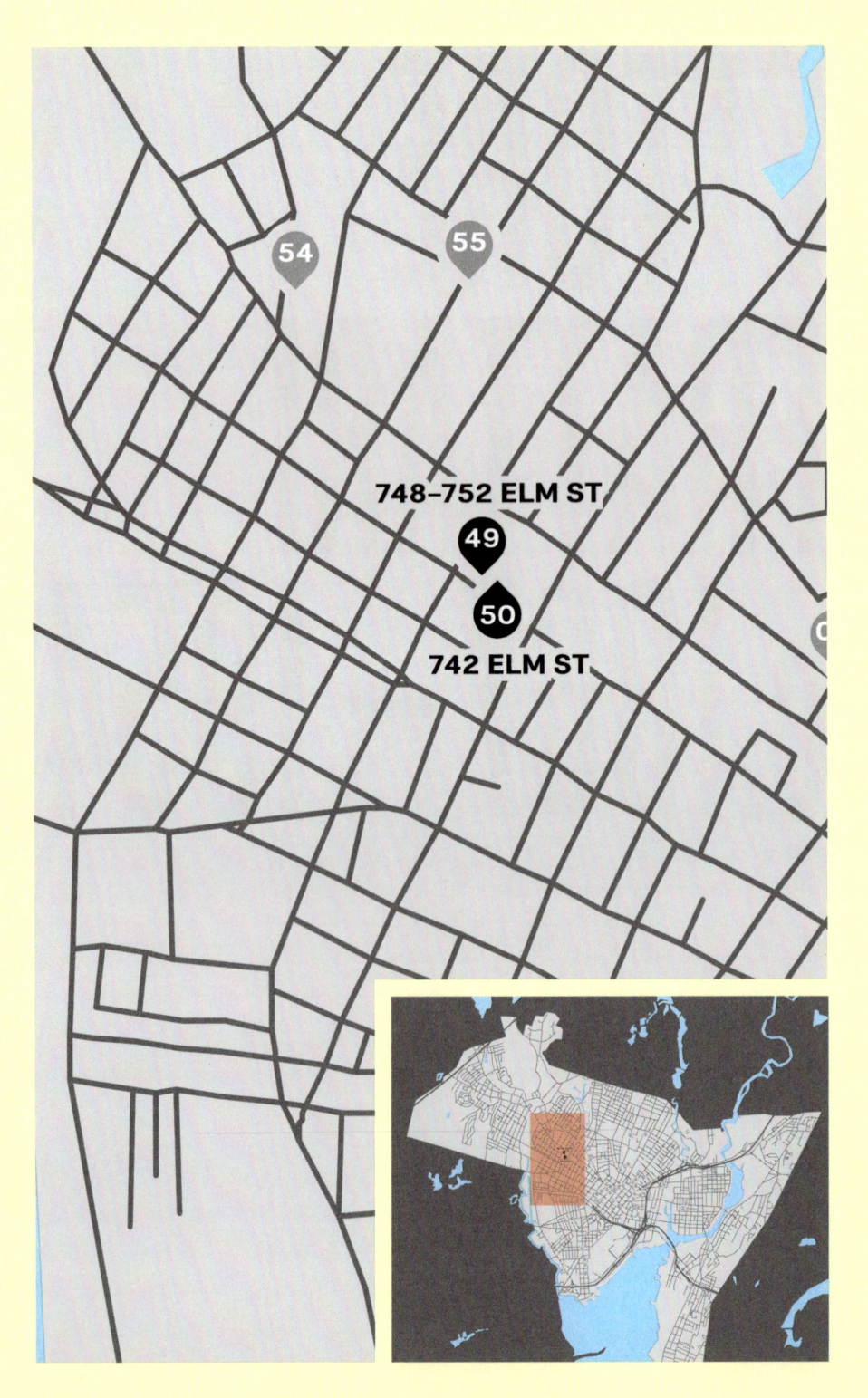

748–752 Elm Street

50

742 Elm Street

Ettore Frattari was born in Italy around 1867. Little is known about his arrival in the United States or how he met his wife, Josephine, also an Italian immigrant. They had six children and lived at 257 Oak Street, where the 1909 City Directory lists him as a tavern keeper. The Oak Street area was a gritty working-class neighborhood that was the first point of entry for many European immigrants to New Haven. Despite its time-worn storefronts, it was a congenial melting-pot where many nationalities and races shared cultures and traditions.

Frattari became a United States citizen and registered with the military in 1917. He was still listed at 257 Oak Street in the 1940 Census, at 73 years old. Frattari died in New Haven in 1954.

In 1909, Frattari built a cluster of distinctive houses on Elm Street near Norton as investment properties. He left no record as to how these houses were financed.

The large house at 748–750 Elm, probably from plans drawn by the firm of Bailey & D'Avino, sweeps around the corner with a generous wrap-around porch marked by a deep cornice and a dozen round columns mounted on the porch railing. With arched windows and bay windows on both sides, the house shows off Frattari's carpentry skills. Attic dormers on both the Elm and Norton sides with oversized semi-circular fans above tripartite windows are a dramatic feature, even on a house with many eye-catching highlights.

A second residence in the same structure (195 Norton Street) is entered under a pediment which neatly terminates the dramatic porch.

The house at 742 Elm Street, constructed a short while later, maintains the same assured level of detail with a semi-circular porch with flared steps and chunky columns, double-height bay windows, and a leaded oval window. The door to a former second-story porch retains its original fanlight and sidelights. The corners of the house are dressed with paneled pilasters. Both 742 Elm and 748 Elm smoothly combine a variety of decorative elements.

The house at 746 Elm has been sided, covering details such as the cornice and corner pilasters, but has the same overall structure as 742 Elm.

The generous front set-backs and spacious porches on these houses represent new "suburban" housing models, as the City's middle class population moved toward Westville in the early twentieth century.

ALICE T. WASHBURN 1870–1958

52 30 ALSTON AVE
51 86 ELMWOOD RD
53 11 ALDEN AVE

51 · 86 Elmwood Road

52 · 30 Alston Avenue

171 ALICE T. WASHBURN

11 Alden Avenue

Nearly 90 houses in New Haven, Hamden and Cheshire were designed by Alice Washburn, a self-taught builder/architect who began with small "spec" houses of her own design in the Spring Glen neighborhood of Hamden and specialized in gracious custom-built homes. Born in 1870, she was a school teacher, wife, and mother who did not begin her career in construction until she was 49. Relegated to obscurity for decades after her death, admiration for her talent as a designer has steadily grown since 1990.

Alice Frances Trythall was born in Cheshire and was trained as a teacher. She married Edward M. Washburn in 1896 and had two daughters. Family stories say Washburn felt that women were best qualified to design houses since they were typically in charge of domestic life. Her decision to enter the business world as a designer and builder occurred just as the suburbs of New Haven experienced a building boom in the 1920s. For a decade, Washburn's designs were in great demand for their appealing style and workmanship.

She was known for her close supervision of every facet of the construction process, including interior design. Washburn had a permanent crew of carpenters and craftsmen who executed most of her designs as a team. The loyalty and skill of the team she assembled contributed significantly to her work. Washburn insisted on a level of

Family stories say Washburn felt that women were best qualified to design houses since they were typically in charge of domestic life. Her decision to enter the business world as a designer and builder occurred just as the suburbs of New Haven experienced a building boom in the 1920s. For a decade, Washburn's designs were in great demand for their appealing style and workmanship.

quality and built accordingly, even if the owner could not pay for a feature Washburn wanted. When she added unasked-for features to suit her design standards, she would occasionally not charge the client for them.

There are ten Washburn houses in New Haven, built between 1924 and 1930. An example at 11 Alden Avenue is noticeable for its broad doorway framed with complex details: matching sets of triple pilasters topped by heavy cornices with a fan light squeezed between them.

On a nearby street in Westville, 30 Alston Avenue is larger than most Washburn houses in New Haven, with a side wing. This doorway is also richly ornamented, with a classic pediment, shallow arched window over the door, and decorative glass in the side panels.

The house at 86 Elmwood Road exhibits some characteristic features but is unusual in other ways. The large windows, corner pilasters, and ground level entryway are seen in many Washburn designs. However, 86 Elmwood is asymmetrical, with a projecting section of the façade placed off-center, creating a more dynamic look in lieu of Washburn's typical symmetry.

This house has a cross-gable roofline, responding to its corner location, and two architecturally distinct entrances, one with a pedimented hood and the other with a flat roof supported by round columns. Washburn's insistence on making the whole property architecturally consistent is demonstrated by formal columns matching the porch columns flanking the doors of the detached garage.

Her refusal to compromise on building details she felt were important, along with her lack of business experience, were factors in her inability to withstand the Depression, and her business closed in 1931. She died in 1958, unremarked except by family and members of her longstanding crew of craftsmen.

Washburn had the ability to give lasting character to domestic architecture and left a portfolio of elegant and visually satisfying houses. Over the last 30 years, a detailed monograph, media coverage, and walking tours have found a new generation of admirers for her work.

VITO ZICHICHI 1876–1951

54 13-33 BLAKE ST

55 409 ELLSWORTH AVE

49

50

13–15, 17–19, 21–23, 27–29, and 31–33 Blake Street

21–23 Blake Street

179　VITO ZICHICHI

55 409 Ellsworth Avenue

Vito Zichichi was born in 1876 and immigrated to New Haven in 1907 with his wife, Concetta. They lived at 10 Prince Street in 1908 soon after their arrival, and at 104 Congress Avenue beginning in 1920. Zichichi died in 1951 at the age of 74.

Zichichi was a "joiner" by trade but had resources that enabled him to become a modest real estate developer. In early twentieth century, the area north of Whalley Avenue and west of the Boulevard was opened up for development. A developer named John J. Linskey bought land and laid out 48 building lots called Fairlawn Manor in a corridor between Blake Street and the Boulevard. These parcels would have been considered the country and appealed to homebuyers leaving denser areas of the City.

In 1915 Zichichi built five houses at the southern edge of Fairlawn Manor, at numbers 13–15, 17–19, 21–23, 27–29 and 31–33 Blake Street, based on plans drawn by architect C. Jerome Bailey. Zichichi sold them for $6,000 each. The five Blake Street houses are almost identical, with intersecting cross-gable roofs, side-hall entries, and clusters of columns framing the porches. This type of two-family dwelling, with flats on the first and second floors, was a common housing type in early twentieth century New Haven. Zichichi's houses have more carpentry detail than many houses of this type, especially in the eave and porch trim.

In 1920 Zichichi built the stylish house at 409 Ellsworth Avenue and sold it for $12,000. A particularly spacious and elaborate example of the two-family house type, it has many delicate carpentry details, especially in the porch trim and window treatment. The wide sidelights at the entry echo several leaded glass panes beside and above the second-floor window. The enclosed second-story porch repeats the motif of broad fan windows under a crisp cornice. Clapboard skirts on the sides of the second story flare out subtly, giving the house a three-dimensional effect.

This house was built a block from land owned by the Beaver Hills Company, which laid out one of the largest planned developments in New Haven. Between 1908 and 1938, the developers sold building lots along their new streets, offering buyers a variety of house types. The company was among the first to maintain standards of design at a large scale. Beaver Hills houses north of Goffe Street along Ellsworth, Norton, and Winthrop Avenues remain desirable today. Zichichi's house at 409 Ellsworth, although a bit south of the corporate Beaver Hills project, holds its own as an attractive addition to the neighborhood.

INDEX

PAGE   BUILDER

17   Nahum Hayward

143 Elm Street

46 Hillhouse Avenue

Fence around the Green

25   Elihu Atwater

31   William Lanson

39   Simeon Jocelyn

Street Building
742 Chapel Street

Long Wharf Pier

Fence around
Trowbridge Square

47   Atwater Treat

32 Walnut Street and
Jocelyn Square

Goffe Street School
106 Goffe Street

Exchange Building
121 Church Street

55   Sidney Mason Stone

250 Church Street

37–39 Wooster Place

311 Temple Street

184   THE BUILDER BOOK   NEW HAVEN PRESERVATION TRUST

PAGE   BUILDER

55   Sidney Mason Stone (cont.)

169 Olive Street

55 Hillhouse Avenue

65   Stephen Perkins

1032 Chapel Street

Trinity Chapel
301 George Street

Street Hall
1071 Chapel Street

393 Prospect Street

73   James E. English

9 Wooster Place

592 Chapel Street

81   Philo Chatfield

66 Lyon Street

89   Massena Clark

254 Greene Street

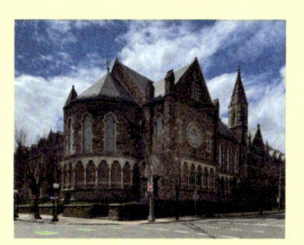

Battell Chapel
400 College Street

86 Hallock Street

185   INDEX

PAGE   BUILDER

89   Massena Clark (cont.)

315 St. Ronan Street

97   Willis M. Smith

399 Orange Street

Wolf's Head
77 Prospect Street

105   Nehemiah D. Sperry

Soldiers and Sailors
Monument, East Rock Park

466 Orange Street

42 Academy Street

115   Arthur B. Treat

405–415 Orange Street

28–36 Trumbull Street

466 Howard Avenue

123   Lyman V. Treat & George M. Treat

37 High Street

840 Howard Avenue

836 Howard Avenue

PAGE BUILDER

129 George P. Merwin

22 Eld Street

938 Grand Avenue
(135–139 Olive Street)

135 George A. Baldwin

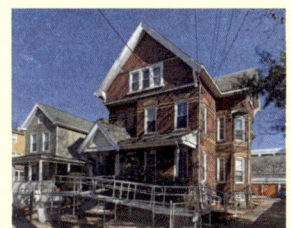

297 Howard Avenue

333 Howard Avenue

217 Howard Avenue

143 Charles M. McLinn

Farnam Hall
380 College Street

Durfee Hall
198 Elm Street

149 George Bohn

Quinnipiac Brewery
21 River Street

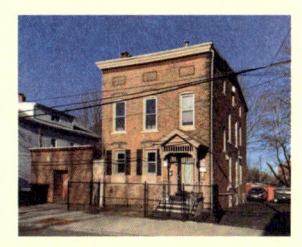

21 Kossuth Street

157 Thomas F. Lowe

338–340 Grand Avenue

342–346 Grand Avenue

350 Grand Avenue

187   INDEX

PAGE   BUILDER

163 Ettore Frattari

748–752 Elm Street

742 Elm Street

169 Alice T. Washburn

86 Elmwood Road

30 Alston Avenue

11 Alden Avenue

177 Vito Zichichi

13–15, 17–19, 21–23, 27–29 and 31–33 Blake Street

409 Ellsworth Avenue

SOURCES

PAGE

17 Nahum Hayward

Atwater, Edward E., ed. *History of the City of New Haven to the Present Time*. New York: W.W. Munsell and Company, 1887, p. 551.

Blake, Henry Taylor. *Chronicles of New Haven Green from 1638 to 1862; a series of papers read before the New Haven Colony Historical Society*.

Brown, Elizabeth Mills. *New Haven; A Guide to Architecture and Urban Design*. New Haven: Yale University Press, 1976. pp. 5, 104–105, 141.

Connecticut Herald, June 17, 1834.

Connecticut State Library, "The CT Annual Register and U.S. Calendar," for the political year 1839.

Dana, Arnold Guyot. "Pictorial New Haven, Old and New." Unpublished Scrapbooks. New Haven Museum Library, New Haven, CT. Vol. 32.5, pp. 106–109.

Kelley, Brooks M. *An Area of Historic Houses on Hillhouse Avenue and Trumbull Street*. New Haven Preservation Trust, 1974, pp. 12–16 (re Sachem's Wood and Skinner House).

New Haven Preservation Trust. *New Haven Historic Resources Inventory*. Bound collection, 1981.

Family Search database. [https://familysearch.org]

Find a Grave: https://www.findagrave.com/memorial/11389156/nahum-hayward

25 Elihu Atwater

Atwater, Edward E., ed. *History of the City of New Haven to the Present Time*. New York: W.W. Munsell and Company, 1887. p. 551.

Brown, Elizabeth Mills. *New Haven; A Guide to Architecture and Urban Design*. New Haven: Yale University Press, 1976. pp. 5, 117.

Caplan, Colin M. *A Guide to Historic New Haven Connecticut*. Charleston, S.C.: The History Press, 2007, p. 26.

Connecticut Digital Archive: *Connecticut Annual Register and United States Calendar*, 1835 and 1839.

Connecticut Digital Archive: Jerome B. Lucke, *History of the New Haven Grays from September 1816 to September 1876*. Tuttle, Morehouse & Taylor, 1876. [http://hdl.handle.net/11134/30002:5338029]

Dana, Arnold Guyot. "Pictorial New Haven, Old and New." Unpublished Scrapbooks. New Haven Museum Library, New Haven, CT. Vol. 5, p. 45.

New Haven Preservation Trust. *New Haven Historic Resources Inventory*. Bound collection, 1981.

Family Search database. [https://familysearch.org]

31 William Lanson

Brown, Elizabeth Mills. *New Haven; A Guide to Architecture and Urban Design*. New Haven: Yale University Press, 1976. pp. 13, 24 (re Long Wharf Pier).

Clouette, Bruce. *Historical and Archaeological Assessment Survey: Long Wharf Pier Structure*. Report prepared by Architectural and Historical Services, Inc.: 2008.

Highsmith, Gary. *William Lanson, New Haven's African King*. Curriculum Unit 97.04.04, Yale-New Haven Teacher's Institute. New Haven, 1997.

Hinks, Peter B.. *The Successes and Struggles of New Haven Entrepreneur William Lanson*. CT Humanities, 2021. [http://www.Connecticut History.org].

39 Simeon Jocelyn

Brooklyn Eagle, August 20, 1879.

Brown, Elizabeth Mills. *New Haven; A Guide to Architecture and Urban Design*. New Haven: Yale University Press, 1976. pp. 94, 173, 194.

Dana, Arnold Guyot. "Pictorial New Haven, Old and New." Unpublished Scrapbooks. New Haven Museum Library, New Haven, CT. Vol. 66, pp. 43–49.

McQueeny, Mary Beth. "Simeon Jocelyn, New Haven Reformer." Journal of the N.H. Colony Historical Society, Vol. 19, No. 3. 1970.

New Haven Museum. Microfilm 1-C, Reel 7, Frame 6. Obituary in unidentified newspaper.

Penar, Dorothea & J. Paul Loether. *National Register of Historic Places Nomination Form: Trowbridge Square Historic District*. National Park Service, 1985.

"Simeon Jocelyn," entry in undated website Yale, Slavery, and Abolition. Yale University. [http://www.yaleslavery.org/Abolitionsts/abolit.html]

U.S. Census: 1850, 1860, 1870.

Family Search database: *Connecticut Marriages, 1630–1997*. (re Harriet Starr, 1822). [https://familysearch.org/ark:/61903/1:1:F7GJ-YL8 : 11 January 2020].

---

47 Atwater Treat

Brown, Elizabeth Mills. *New Haven; A Guide to Architecture and Urban Design*. New Haven: Yale University Press, 1976. pp. 5, 112.

Connecticut State Library: *Green's Connecticut Annual Register and U.S. Calendar for 1847*.

Connecticut State Library: *Resolves and Private Laws of the State of Connecticut, Vol. IV, 1836–1857*.

Connecticut State Library: *New Haven Daily Palladium,* March 27–28, 1862.

Dana, Arnold Guyot. "Pictorial New Haven, Old and New." Unpublished Scrapbooks. New Haven Museum Library, New Haven, CT. Vol. 5, p. 61; Vol. 3 p. 21–31; Vol. 21, pp. 97–110.

Hawes, Rev. Edward. *Funeral Sermon: A Sermon preached on occasion of the death of Deacon Atwater Treat,* April 2, 1882. New Haven: Yale University Library.

New Haven Daily Morning Journal and Courier, multiple issues.

New Haven Museum. Grave Records, Ref. F104.N6, H244. [Headstone Inscriptions, Town of New Haven, from the Charles R. Hale Collection of Headstone Inscriptions, recorded 1932–1934.]

New Haven Preservation Trust. *New Haven Historic Resources Inventory*. Bound collection, 1981.

The Ethnic Heritage Center. *Walk New Haven: Goffe Street Special School for Colored Children and Prince Hall Grand Lodge of Masons*. [http://www.ethnicheritagecenter.org]

55 Sidney Mason Stone

Brown, Elizabeth Mills. *New Haven; A Guide to Architecture and Urban Design*. New Haven: Yale University Press, 1976. pp. 5–6, 106, 142, 187, 193.

Brown, Elizabeth Mills. *The Historic Houses of Wooster Square*. New Haven Preservation Trust, 1969. pp. 114–115.

Dana, Arnold Guyot. "Pictorial New Haven, Old and New." Unpublished Scrapbooks. New Haven Museum Library, New Haven, CT. Vol. 23, pp. 21 and 23, referencing notes by W.G. Snow.

Kelley, Brooks M. *An Area of Historic Houses on Hillhouse Avenue and Trumbull Street*. New Haven Preservation Trust, 1974. pp. 39–41; 74.

Loether, J. Paul. *National Register of Historic Places Nomination Form: Upper State Street*. National Park Service, 1984.

McNicol, Nancy. "Stone Turned," *The Daily Nutmeg*, April 17, 2021.

New Haven Preservation Trust. *New Haven Historic Resources Inventory*. Bound collection, 1981.

Seymour, George Dudley. *New Haven*. Published by the author, 1942.

65 Stephen P. Perkins

Atwater, Edward E., ed. *History of the City of New Haven to the Present Time*. New York: W.W. Munsell and Company, 1887. p. 604.

Brown, Elizabeth Mills. *New Haven; A Guide to Architecture and Urban Design*. New Haven: Yale University Press, 1976. p. 150.

Carroll, Richard C., ed. *Buildings and Grounds of Yale University*, 3rd Edition. New Haven: 1979.

Historic American Buildings Survey (HABS) – Connecticut. National Park Service, 1964.

New Haven Daily Morning Journal and Courier. September, 1890.

New Haven Preservation Trust. *New Haven Historic Resources Inventory*. Bound collection, 1981.

Ryan, Susan. *National Register of Historic Places Nomination Form: Prospect Hill Historic District*. National Park Service, 1979.

Find a Grave: https://www.findagrave.com/memorial/236667941/stephen-p-perkins

73   James E. English

Brown, Elizabeth Mills. *New Haven; A Guide to Architecture and Urban Design*. New Haven: Yale University Press, 1976. pp. 182–183, 186.

Brown, Elizabeth Mills. *The Historic Houses of Wooster Square*. New Haven Preservation Trust, 1969. pp. 62–63; 106–107.

Caplan, Colin M. *A Guide to Historic New Haven Connecticut*. Charleston, S.C.: The History Press, 2007, p. 53.

Commemorative Biographical Record of New Haven County. Chicago: J.H. Beers & Co., 1902.

Dana, Arnold Guyot. "Pictorial New Haven, Old and New." Unpublished Scrapbooks. New Haven Museum Library, New Haven, CT. Vol. 1, p. 23; Vol. 5, pp. 54–54B; and Vol. 63, p.83.

English, Anna Morris. *In Memoriam, James E. English*. Private Printing, 1891. New Haven Museum, MSS 133, Box 4, Folder A.

New Haven Daily Morning Journal and Courier, multiple issues.

New Haven Preservation Trust. *New Haven Historic Resources Inventory*. Bound collection, 1981.

Osterweis, Rollin. *Three Centuries of New Haven, 1638–1938*. New Haven: Yale University Press, 1953.

Sterner, Daniel. *Historic Buildings of Connecticut*. [http://www.historicbuildingsct.com]

U.S. Government Printing Office. *Biographical Directory of the United States Congress, 1774–2005*. [https://www.govinfo.gov/content/pkg/GPO-CDOC-108hdoc222/pdf/GPO-CDOC-108hdoc222.pdf]

Waterbury Evening Democrat. March 3, 1890.

81   Philo Chatfield

Atwater, Edward E., ed. *History of the City of New Haven to the Present Time*. New York: W.W. Munsell and Company, 1887. p. 605.

Brown, Elizabeth Mills. *New Haven; A Guide to Architecture and Urban Design*. New Haven: Yale University Press, 1976. pp. 123–124.

Brown, Elizabeth Mills. *The Historic Houses of Wooster Square*. New Haven Preservation Trust, 1969. pp. 82–83.

Carroll, Richard C., ed. *Buildings and Grounds of Yale University*, 3rd Edition. New Haven: 1979.

Luyster, Constance. *National Register of Historic Places Nomination Form: Wooster Square Historic District*. National Park Service, 1970.

New Haven Preservation Trust. *New Haven Historic Resources Inventory*. Bound collection, 1981.

Osterweis, Rollin. *Three Centuries of New Haven, 1638–1938*. New Haven: Yale University Press, 1953.

Ransom, David F. and John Herzan. *National Register of Historic Places Nomination Form: East Rock Park*. National Park Service, 1976.

Family Search database. [https://familysearch.org]
Find a Grave: https://www.familysearch.org/ark:/61903/1:1:QV22-JSW3

---

89 Massena Clark

Brown, Elizabeth Mills. *New Haven; A Guide to Architecture and Urban Design*. New Haven: Yale University Press, 1976. p. 97.

Connecticut Digital Archive: New Haven Historic District Commission "Study Report: St. Ronan-Edgehill Historic District," April 2008. [http://hdl.handle.net/11134/470002:88201]

Dana, Arnold Guyot. "Pictorial New Haven, Old and New." Unpublished Scrapbooks. New Haven Museum Library, New Haven, CT. Vol. 62, p. 46–48; Vol. 15, p. 76.

Hill, Everett Gleason. *A Modern History of New Haven and Eastern New Haven County*, pp. 108–109. New York: The S.J. Clarke Publishing Co., 1918.

New Haven Daily Morning Journal and Courier, multiple issues.

New Haven Preservation Trust. *New Haven Historic Resources Inventory*. Bound collection, 1981.

Family Search database. [https://familysearch.org]

---

97 Willis Minor Smith

Atwater, Edward E., ed. *History of the City of New Haven to the Present Time*. New York: W.W. Munsell and Company, 1887. pp. 406–407.

Brown, Elizabeth Mills. *New Haven; A Guide to Architecture and Urban Design*. New Haven: Yale University Press, 1976. p. 33.

New Haven Daily Morning Journal and Courier, multiple issues.

New Haven Museum. B13 (Judge Livingston Warner Cleaveland Papers), Reel 2, Volume c-1, pp. 68, 80–82.

New Haven Preservation Trust. *New Haven Historic Resources Inventory*. Bound collection, 1981.

Ransom, David F. *Connecticut's Civil War Monuments*. Connecticut Historical Commission Survey, 1997.

Strahan, Derek. "Wolf's Head Hall, New Haven, Connecticut." *Lost New England*, 2019. [https://lostnewengland.com/2019/08/wolfs-head-hall-new-haven-connecticut]

Family Search database. https://www.familysearch.org/ark:/61903/1:1:QK1K-VNRN

105 Nehemiah Day Sperry

Atwater, Edward E., ed. *History of the City of New Haven to the Present Time*. New York: W.W. Munsell and Company, 1887. p. 382.

Brown, Elizabeth Mills. *New Haven; A Guide to Architecture and Urban Design*. New Haven: Yale University Press, 1976. pp. 33, 157–158, 161, 189.

Commemorative Biographical Record of New Haven County. Chicago: J.H. Beers & Co., 1902. p. 36.

New Haven Preservation Trust. *New Haven Historic Resources Inventory*. Bound collection, 1981.

Penar, Dorothea, J. Paul Loether, and John Herzan. *National Register of Historic Places Nomination Form: Orange Street Historic District*. National Park Service, 1985.

Ransom, David F. *Connecticut's Civil War Monuments*. Connecticut Historical Commission Survey, 1997.

Find a Grave: https://www.findagrave.com/memorial/12649480/nehemiah-day-sperry

115   Arthur Barnes Treat

Atwater, Edward E., ed. *History of the City of New Haven to the Present Time*. New York: W.W. Munsell and Company, 1887. pp. 605–606

Commemorative Biographical Record of New Haven County. Chicago: J.H. Beers & Co., 1902. pp. 601–03.

New Haven Preservation Trust. *New Haven Historic Resources Inventory*. Bound collection, 1981.

Find a Grave: https://www.findagrave.com/memorial/147400878/arthur-barnes-treat

123   Lyman V. Treat and George M. Treat

Brown, Elizabeth Mills. *New Haven; A Guide to Architecture and Urban Design*. New Haven: Yale University Press, 1976. p. 88.

City Directories

New Haven Daily Morning Journal and Courier, multiple issues.

New Haven Preservation Trust. *New Haven Historic Resources Inventory*. Bound collection, 1981.

U.S. Census: 1860, 1870, 1880

Find a Grave: https://www.familysearch.org/ark:/61903/1:1:QK1K-VPFQ

129   George Platt Merwin

Atwater, Edward E., ed. *History of the City of New Haven to the Present Time*. New York: W.W. Munsell and Company, 1887. p. 553.

Caplan, Colin M. *A Guide to Historic New Haven Connecticut*. Charleston, S.C.: The History Press, 2007, p. 85.

City Directories

Commemorative Biographical Record of New Haven County. Chicago: J.H. Beers & Co., 1902. p. 1434.

New Haven Preservation Trust. *New Haven Historic Resources Inventory*. Bound collection, 1981.

Family Search database. [https://familysearch.org]

Find a Grave: https://www.findagrave.com/memorial/147385556/george-platt-merwin

135 George A. Baldwin

Atwater, Edward E., ed. *History of the City of New Haven to the Present Time.* New York: W.W. Munsell and Company, 1887. p. 605.

Baldwin, Charles Candee. *The Baldwin Genealogy from 1500 to 1881,* Cleveland, Ohio 1881.

City Directories: 1870 and 1887.

Jerome B. Lucke scrapbook, New Haven Museum, B27, Box 11, Folder A.

New Haven Daily Morning Journal and Courier, multiple issues.

New Haven Preservation Trust. New Haven Historic Resources Inventory. Bound collection, 1981.

U.S. Census, 1880

Find a Grave Index, https://www.familysearch.org/ark/61903/1:1:QK1K-J6FR

143 Charles M. McLinn

Carroll, Richard C., ed. *Buildings and Grounds of Yale University,* 3rd Edition. New Haven: 1979.

My Heritage Family Trees. [https://www.myheritage.com]

New Haven Daily Morning Journal and Courier, multiple issues.

Warner, Charles Jr. *The Yale and Slavery Research Project.* Yale University, 2021. [https://yaleandslavery.yale.edu]

Yale-New Haven Teachers Institute. "20th Century Afro-American Culture." Vol. II, Unit 6, 1978.

Find a Grave database. [https://www.findagrave.com/memorial/145730843/charles-mclinn].

149 George Bohn

Caplan, Colin M. *A Guide to Historic New Haven Connecticut.* Charleston, S.C.: The History Press, 2007, p. 61.

Commemorative Biographical Record of New Haven County. Chicago: J.H. Beers & Co., 1902. p. 1543.

Connecticut Naturalization Records. https://www.familysearch.org/ark/61903/1:1:ZXVQ-S83Z

Dana, Arnold Guyot. "Pictorial New Haven, Old and New." Unpublished Scrapbooks. New Haven Museum Library, New Haven, CT. Vol. 123.5, p. 61.

New Haven Daily Morning Journal and Courier, multiple issues.

New Haven Preservation Trust. *New Haven Historic Resources Inventory*. Bound collection, 1981.

Roth, Matthew, Bruce Clouette, and John Herzan. *National Register of Historic Places Nomination Form: Quinnipiac Brewery*. National Park Service, 1982.

U.S. Census: 1900

Find a Grave: https://www.familysearch.org/ark/61903/1:1:QK1K-J6P7

157 Thomas Lowe

Atwater, Edward E., ed. *History of the City of New Haven to the Present Time*. New York: W.W. Munsell and Company, 1887. p, 554.

Caplan, Colin M. *A Guide to Historic New Haven Connecticut*. Charleston, S.C.: The History Press, 2007, p. 168.

New Haven Museum. Grave Ref. 104.N6 H244 v.3, p. 798. [Headstone Inscriptions, Town of New Haven, from the Charles R. Hale Collection of Headstone Inscriptions (recorded 1932–1934).]

New Haven Preservation Trust. *New Haven Historic Resources Inventory*. Bound collection, 1981.

U.S. Census: 1880

163 Ettore Frattari

Caplan, Colin M. *A Guide to Historic New Haven Connecticut*. Charleston, S.C.: The History Press, 2007, p. 74.

City Directories: 1908, 1909, 1910, 1950, 1954.

New Haven Preservation Trust. *New Haven Historic Resources Inventory*. Bound collection, 1981.

Riccio, Anthony V. *The Italian American Experience in New Haven*. State University of New York, 2006.

U.S. Census: 1940, 1950.

Family Search database. "Connecticut, Military Census Questionnaires, 1917." [https://www.familysearch.org/ark:/61903/1:1:ZVYK-CTW2.]

169 Alice T. Washburn

Hitchcock, Charlotte R. *Alice Washburn: Westville Walking Tour Guide*. New Haven Preservation Trust, 1990.

New Haven Preservation Trust. *New Haven Historic Resources Inventory*. Bound collection, 1981.

Yellig, Martha Finder. *Alice Washburn Architect* (Monograph). Hamden, CT: Tiger Lily Press, 1990.

177 Vito Zichichi

Caplan, Colin M. *A Guide to Historic New Haven Connecticut*. Charleston, S.C.: The History Press, 2007, p. 93.

Connecticut Death Index, 1949–2001. FamilySearch database. [https://familysearch.org/ark:/61903/1:1:VZPY-9F1 : 9 December 2014].

Dana, Arnold Guyot. "Pictorial New Haven, Old and New." Unpublished Scrapbooks. New Haven Museum Library, New Haven, CT.

Herzan, John and J. Paul Loether. *State Register of Historic Places Nomination Form: Fairlawn-Nettleton Historic District*. Connecticut State Historic Preservation Office, 2005.

New Haven Preservation Trust. *New Haven Historic Resources Inventory*. Bound collection, 1981.

U.S. Census: 1920